Gage Canadian Writer's Handbook

Richard Davies
Glen Kirkland

gage EDUCATIONAL PUBLISHING COMPANY
A DIVISION OF CANADA PUBLISHING CORPORATION
Vancouver · Calgary · Toronto · London · Halifax

We acknowledge the financial support of the Government of Canada through the Book Publishing Industry Development Program for our publishing activities.

Reviewers and Consultants
Francine Artichuk, District 02/04, NB
Janet Barkhouse, Southwest Regional School Board, NS
Alice Carlson, Durham District School Board, ON
Graham Foster, Calgary Catholic School District, AB
June James, School District 36, BC
Helen MacDonell, Southwest Regional School Board, NS
Cam Macpherson, Toronto District School Board, ON
Elaine Sokoloski, Edmonton Catholic School Board, AB

Gage wishes to acknowledge the contributions of Angelo Bolotta, Chelsea Donaldson, Todd Mercer, Greg Robinson, and John Watson.

With a special thank you to Kevin Kirkland, and to Karen, Heather, and Scott Davies.

Canadian Cataloguing in Publication Data

Davies, Richard
    Gage Canadian writer's handbook
    ISBN 0-7715-1747-5
    1. English language – Composition and exercises. 2. Essay – Authorship.
    3. English language – Grammar. I. Kirkland, Glen. II. Title. III. Title:
    Canadian writer's handbook.
    PE1408.D384 2000   808'.042   C99-932916-2

We hope you find this handbook helpful, informative, and easy to use.
If you have any comment that will help us improve our next edition
of this book, please let our editorial team know.
Gage Educational Publishing Company
164 Commander Blvd.
Toronto, ON M1S 3C7
fax   416-293-0757
e-mail info@gagelearning.com

Publisher, secondary education: Janice Schoening
Editorial team: Carol Waldock, Eileen Brett
Cover and page design: Fizz Design Inc.

ISBN 0-7715-1747-5

1 2 3 4 5 FP 04 03 02 01 00

Written, Printed, and Bound in Canada

Table of Contents

Introduction

Writing a good essay is not easy. Like all skills, it takes practice, preparation, organization, focus, and experience. Most successful people do not achieve their success without a combination of all of these qualities. Having said that, it is also true that *anyone* — regardless of skill or knowledge background — can learn to write a better essay. And that is what this handbook is all about.

Want to go through the stages of writing an essay from scratch? That's what Part 1 is about. Want some help in writing a review? See Part 2. Want to sort out confusing sets of words (for example, *their-they're-there*)? Go to the pages with the coloured edges, in Part 3.

Read the Contents (or the index at the back of the book) if you know what your specific topic or writing need is. You will not have to look too far to find what you require in this compact, hands-on resource.

Good luck with your writing assignments.

Richard Davies, Glen Kirkland

Ten Ways to Improve Your Writing

1. Do your assigned homework reading. Read all handouts carefully, and write down all information put on the board by your teacher. Ask questions to clarify any uncertainties about your assignments.

2. Make use of available study guides and critical studies of works discussed in class. This is especially important in literature classes.

3. Listen carefully and thoughtfully. Always have a pen in hand, taking notes during discussions: selection titles, author, character names, key plot/conflict details, information about character, symbol, and theme. Review and study these notes for quizzes, test essays, and exams.

4. Ask questions about anything you don't understand discussed in class. Look up unfamiliar words in the dictionary. It's difficult to do well if you don't know the words you are reading, or can't paraphrase correctly what the author is communicating.

5. Ask questions about instructions for assignments. Make sure you're answering the question asked or are responding to key words and all parts of an essay topic. If unsure, discuss the topic with your teacher *before* you start to write.

6. Develop a plan before you write your good copy. Do as many drafts as you can before writing the final copy.

7. **Before submitting an assignment, have several people read it over.**
   Ask your readers to check the following:

   - **content:** "Do I have enough ideas and examples? What can be added or deleted?" It may be necessary for your reader to know the selection to get *good* feedback on content.

   - **organization:** "Have I got a thesis, topic sentences, introduction, conclusion, a title? Is my material in the best order? Have I organized by selection? character? idea? main events?"

   - **sentences:** "Are they clear and complete? (Remember, simpler is better.) Are the verb tenses in agreement? Is there anything that sounds awkward?"

   - **word choice:** "Is my word choice clear and specific? Have I maintained an appropriate formal tone? Have I avoided using 'they,' 'you,' 'I,' and slang?"

   - **spelling:** "Is my spelling accurate?"

   - **apostrophes and other punctuation:** "Have I correctly used punctuation marks?"

   - **legibility:** "Is my work legible/readable?"

8. **Read over teacher comments,** not just the marks. What are you doing well? What do you need to change or improve? Your main writing problems will usually be obvious after one to two pieces of writing.

9. **For spelling errors,** get a scribbler and divide each page into two columns. Write the error on one side and the correction on the other. Review this list of misspelled words before every test and before you turn in assignments.

10. **Do all the rewrites** and ask for/suggest relevant extra work. Never underestimate the power of practice in English.

Note-Taking Skills

Notes are essentially your written thoughts and understanding of something that you have read, heard, or viewed. Note-taking presupposes good listening skills and attentiveness. At a basic level, you should be able to read or make sense of your own notes. They should summarize the main points and examples of the original learning situation. The important things to remember when making notes are:

- Make it clear which are the major points and which are the minor points.
- Show the relationships among the ideas.
- Note specific examples.
- Write down questions to ask the teacher or presenter.

A simple, but effective system of note-taking is to divide your notes page into two columns. On the left side of the line, put down each of the main ideas being presented. On the right side, put down (in point form) the important details or examples for that same idea or paragraph/section.

One helpful review aspect of the two-column method is that you can fold the page to cover the specific content of the paragraph and show only the ideas or subtopics. If you take time to recall the detail for each idea or subtopic, you will soon know the content of that page of notes.

Example of sequence:

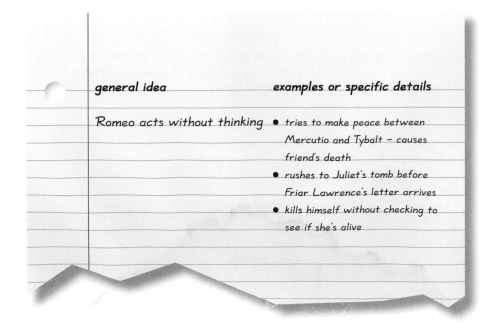

general idea	examples or specific details
Romeo acts without thinking	• tries to make peace between Mercutio and Tybalt – causes friend's death • rushes to Juliet's tomb before Friar Lawrence's letter arrives • kills himself without checking to see if she's alive

One other approach is to use visual organizers such as boxes, arrows, charts, or bubbles to show sequence, development, cause-effect, problem-solution, or other structures in the original learning situation.

Example of sequence:

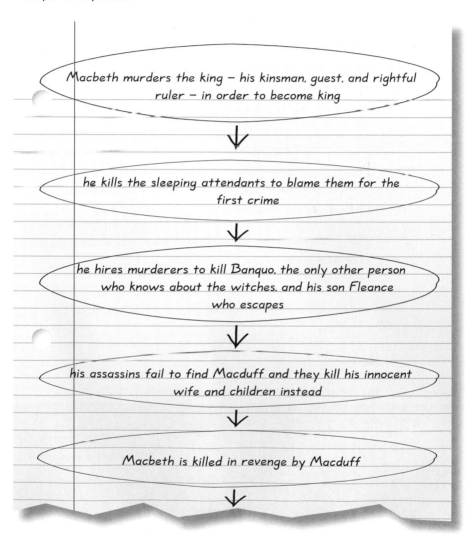

Macbeth murders the king — his kinsman, guest, and rightful ruler — in order to become king

↓

he kills the sleeping attendants to blame them for the first crime

↓

he hires murderers to kill Banquo, the only other person who knows about the witches, and his son Fleance who escapes

↓

his assassins fail to find Macduff and they kill his innocent wife and children instead

↓

Macbeth is killed in revenge by Macduff

↓

Organizing Your Time

Here are some ways that will help you to keep track of your assignments and use your time more efficiently.

- Use a journal or an agenda to keep track of due dates. Get in the habit of looking at your agenda every day.

- Use the amount of time you are given to complete an assignment as a clue to what your teacher expects. If you are assigned a writing project today that is due tomorrow, chances are you will not be expected to do a lot of research or to write a lengthy piece. You will, however, be expected to present ideas that are well thought through, well written, and carefully proofread. On the other hand, if you have a week or more to complete the assignment, budget more time for research or preparation, be prepared to develop your ideas in more detail, and spend more time revising your writing. Whatever the assignment, make sure you understand exactly what is expected, and by when.

- Break down big assignments into smaller tasks, and estimate the amount of time you will need for each stage. For example, if you are writing a research paper, you will probably need to set aside about half the time you have available for the actual research. The other half can be divided among drafting, revising, editing, and proofreading.

- Set aside a particular time and place for assignments and stick to your schedule. Not only will a regular routine help you to concentrate when it is time to work, it will also help you to relax when it isn't.

Part 1

How to Write an Essay

What Are the Essentials of a Good Essay?

Here are the ways English essays are typically judged:

Content: *Insights, ideas, reasons, examples, quotations.*
Be a credible person — know what you're talking about. You have something to say. This comes down to the sense and insight of your ideas as well as your use of appropriate, relevant facts. Give details, provide convincing examples, choose good direct quotations. It's next to impossible to write a good essay if you don't understand the literature you're interpreting, if you distort or misinterpret facts, if you contradict yourself, if you have few points to make, or few examples to give.

Organization: *Parts and sections in logical order.*
Check the overall organization. Make sure the logical development of your ideas falls into distinct sections. Give the reader a clear sense of what you're doing. You have to have a *thesis* (a statement of the essay's main idea or purpose) in the first paragraph. Develop the main idea in such a way that everything ties in with it: introduction, body paragraphs, conclusion. A good essay is focussed: there is no unnecessary repetition, there is clearly a plan, transitions work well, and the whole essay hangs together.

Coherence: *Sentences clear and complete, with good transitions.*
Get your writing into good shape. Write smooth transitions between sections and between sentences. A good essay is coherent — it communicates clearly and significantly about a topic.

Diction: *Interesting, mature word choices.*
Use language appropriate to the situation and to the audience. For instance, you wouldn't need to use the word *I* in a formal essay. Similarly, you wouldn't use insulting nouns or threatening verbs in writing a complaint letter to a business. Be concise. Write exactly what you mean, and use words in a thoughtful, sensitive way to create meaning and understanding. This is obviously an area of growth for most writers and may require more reading, long-term practice, and vocabulary explorations with a dictionary and a thesaurus.

Conventions: *Correct spelling, punctuation, capitalization.*
For many writers, this is the most important area of concern, and there's something to this concern. It *is* difficult to appreciate a writer's ideas when there are several mistakes — mispunctuated sentences, misspelled words, misused capital letters — on every page. Thought and detail are more important than mechanics, *but* people *do* judge on the basis of, for example, legibility and spelling. Appropriate usage and correct grammar can give your writing the final polish of success. A page edited to the satisfaction of approved rules and common standards shows that you have really approached the job in the right way.

Getting Started

Here are ten basic steps to writing an essay.

1. **Understand the assignment instructions**, and focus on what topics are acceptable, or what the limits of a given topic are.

2. **Brainstorm ideas** and examples on the topic, and select subtopics.

3. **Compose an initial (working) thesis,** that is, a sentence stating the main idea.

4. **Add and delete ideas** and specific examples on the basis of their relevance to the thesis and topic.

5. **Organize** the sections and subparts.

6. **Assemble an outline**.

7. **Write at least one draft** or rough copy.

8. **Revise and edit** this draft.

9. **Proofread**.

10. **Produce a neat final copy**.

1. Understand the Topic

Often the topic is given to the student by the teacher. For example, you might be asked to write a personal response on a general topic such as "The Future." In English courses, you are often asked to analyse literature. You might be asked to discuss the storm symbolism in *King Lear*, or to compare and contrast two characters in a selection. (For an example of a prepared essay about literature, see p. 41.) Regardless of what type of essay you are asked to write, there are basic approaches to the writing task.

Let's work with the first topic mentioned above — "The Future" — and assume your English teacher has assigned this as an opening assignment in a unit about the future.

Your teacher has said that you are to write a personal response essay. You have been instructed to discuss three aspects or subtopics in some detail, about different technologies and your views on them. You are also to try to establish if you are generally positive (optimistic) or negative (pessimistic) about the future in general. You have been told that you don't have to do formal research for this topic. (Approaches to the research essay are discussed later on p. 78.) You are to rely on what you already know (prior background knowledge), and have observed.

2. Brainstorm

Brainstorming (by yourself or with others) is simply noting down what you already know and think about a topic. Start by writing down areas or subtopics that come to mind about the topic. These do not have to be in any particular order at this stage.

Ask yourself, "What *about* the future? What do I think it will be like? What are some of the technologies that are developing today which will become common in the future? How might these affect human beings?"

As you can see from these questions, it is best to go step-by-step, thought-by-thought into a topic. Some of the "scattergram" of answers that you might have written down for the above questions will become your starting notes for the essay. A more detailed list of possibilities might look something like the following:

- the future promises many exciting new technologies
- some of these technologies will negatively affect people: e.g. losing jobs to automation
- computers are helpful in education: e.g. helping students to word process; spell checkers, electronic dictionaries (**computers**)
- cloning – creating new species; what for? e.g. Dolly the famous sheep – first famous clone (**cloning**)
- transplanted artificial limbs helpful to amputees
- animal spare parts (**health**)
- robot cats, surgeons; robot soccer; robots in military (**robots**)
- increase in machine-made pollutants; global warming; decline in ozone layer (**environment**)
- intelligent highways; electric cars (**transportation**)

It is important to write down as much as you can at this point to clarify your initial thoughts on the topic. (You can always delete or add other points later.) Even from a modest list such as the above, you can see the range of possibilities for your topic on the future. Some of these are ideas — new technologies can help or can negatively affect people. Others are details — specific references to facts such as Dolly, the first cloned sheep. Try to begin with a fairly balanced list of ideas and details.

Next, use your brainstorming list to indicate related areas or subtopics. (This has been shown in the list above in **boldface**. You might use underlining, brackets, or a different pen colour to make these potential subtopics more obvious to you.)

From your brainstorming list, some possible angles and subtopics begin to emerge:

- computers
- cloning
- health
- robots
- environment
- transportation

Another way to deal with your list is to cluster it:

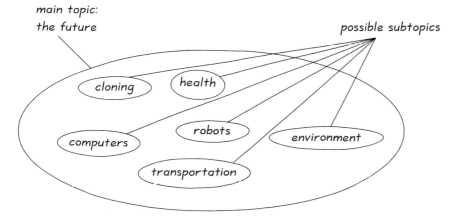

Pick Subtopics

What you have to decide next is which aspects *you* want to focus on. You could, for instance, pick out three areas that you're personally interested in. These might turn out to be a mix of optimistic and pessimistic perspectives:

- usefulness of robots (positive slant)
- cloning tampers with Nature (negative slant)
- technology's harmful effects on the environment (negative slant).

Another approach is to take *one* slant — say, the optimistic view — and focus on three points/areas/potential subtopics you know about:

- computers are helpful in education
- transplanted artificial limbs for amputees
- robots to serve human beings.

Once you have explored your list this far and considered subtopics, you're probably ready to compose an initial (working) thesis.

The discipline of the writer is to learn to be still and listen to what his subject has to tell him.

Rachel Carson

3. Compose the Thesis

It is difficult to write a thesis earlier than this stage for a number of reasons. You have to figure out, first of all, what you know about the topic — this is the purpose of brainstorming. Also, doing a light, preliminary organization of your notes will help you to arrive at what your main slant is likely to be on the topic. At this stage, it is not necessary to have the final wording of your thesis. (More concise rewording may come later in the draft or final copy.) All you need for now is a working thesis which clarifies and focusses your initial position on the topic.

If you have a mixture of opinions, such as in the first case above, then a statement of your views on the topic might be: "Although there are a number of new, positive technologies, other technologies and attitudes toward the environment raise serious concerns about the future." In this example, the *order* of the words "positive" and "concerns" in the thesis will determine how you finally organize the parts of your essay; that is, going from positive views to concerns.

The thesis, obviously, should contain key words from the assignment:

- "technologies," "future" — these words identify the context of this essay

- "Although ... serious concerns" — your assignment is supposed to indicate what you think the effect of these technologies will be, and whether you are optimistic or pessimistic, so this phrase gives an indication of your attitude and clarifies your position.

4. Refine Your List

Having organized a brief list and developed a working thesis, this is a good time to remove information which is irrelevant and no longer required. This is also the logical stage to add more facts, points, examples, reasons, arguments, and opinions to your list, to give you more to work with, that is, expand and illustrate.

First, it is a good idea to create more focus by eliminating the now-redundant information.

Let's work with the original scattergram list for "The Future" essay, back on p. 6.

Put in order, your revised list might now resemble the following:

- the future promises exciting new technologies

- robot cats, surgeons; robot soccer; robots in the military

- cloning — creating new species

- some technologies will negatively affect people

- increase in machine-made pollutants

- decline in the ozone layer

Now you can go on to add as much information and detail as you know or have discussed with others. This is a good point to start a clean page. If you find you have a lot of points and examples to list, it's a good idea to write in columns. Some writers even put each subtopic on a separate page. Write on one side only and then you'll be able to see all your material at a glance.

Another way to deal with a complicated essay is to write the list on separate pages, then using scissors, cut out and mount the information in preferred order, taping the pieces together or mounting them on blank backing pages. (This is the origin of the "CUT" and "PASTE" functions on a computer.) If you have a lot of information, you may be better off with this hands-on approach, because of the limited size of a computer screen.

A longer, refined list with subtopics might look something like the one on the next page.

Robots
- harvesting robots in California
- agricultural revolution – use of laptops by farmers
- robot surgeons (endobots)
- perform surgery inside body
- remove polyps, blockages
- robot cats (Tama)
- developed for elderly in China
- speak to owners (fifty phrases)
- robot soccer
- mechanical players
- Robo Cup in Japan, 1997
- military robot to test clothing
- walks, bends, squats, crawls
- personal robot – fifteen min. battery limit and expensive
- developed in Tokyo

Cloning
- Dolly – lamb cloned in 1997
- breakthrough to improve livestock
- manipulation of DNA
- animal rights concerns
- alternate versions of self
- sex selection for non-medical reasons
- definition of cloning

Global Warming
- because of technology – serious problem
- emissions rise
- doubling of CO_2
- Arctic and Antarctic ozone layers decrease
- in North, decline in landscape (permafrost)
- increasing disruptions
- 100-year turnaround
- increase in skin cancer from radiation
- air conditioners and refrigerators as polluting culprits

5. Organize the Sections and Subparts

Start by looking for possible connections or *transitions*. These may emerge as early as the brainstorming notes in the essay-writing process.

Since you have more negative information (two sections) than positive (one section), it is quite likely that you are more pessimistic than optimistic about the future. The impression you want to leave dictates that the pessimistic information will be in the later body sections, for emphasis.

Always put the major or most important material toward the end of your essay.

One possible arrangement might be as follows:

- robots serving human beings (positive)

- cloning and its dangers (negative)

- the destruction of the environment by technology (negative).

You will notice that the first two subtopics are about adaptations or new species. It would be a *logical transition* to put those two subtopics back-to-back. This will create a smooth flow between two main sections.

Always look for connections between subtopics as this will help you determine order.

Next, decide on an order for the items *within* each section and number these.

Now that you have added information for your essay and have decided on an order, you should recopy the revised plan neatly in outline form. Your teacher may have asked for this anyway.

I write as straight as I can,
just as I walk as straight as
I can, because that is the best
way to get there.

H.G. Wells

6. Assemble the Outline

A concise outline allows you to see your organized ideas and examples at a glance. Some things to keep in mind about outlines:

- Write your thesis at the top of the outline.

- Be sure to include the introduction (and the conclusion) in the outline.

- Make sure all your material is on topic and develops in a logical order.

- Check for weaker, undeveloped sections. Eliminate these sections, or add more ideas and examples to these sections.

- Balance ideas and examples.

Remember that the outline is a tentative blueprint for your draft and your final copy. After the outline, you can still add, delete, or reorganize information in the next stage, called the draft.

PEANUTS reprinted by permission of UNITED FEATURE SYNDICATE, INC.

The following point-form outline on your developing topic illustrates the above features of a good outline.

Questioning Technology for the Future

(thesis) Although there are a number of new positive
technologies available today, other technologies and
attitudes toward the environment raise serious concerns
for the future.

I. Introduction
  A. Thesis
  B. Robots — positive
    technology
  C. Cloning — concerns
    about
  D. Environment — long-
    term effects of
    technology on it

II. Robots
  A. Personal robots
    1. Two-legged functional
      robot in Tokyo
    2. Does simple fix-it jobs
    3. Short battery life
      and costly
  B. Robot cats (Tama)
    1. Talk to elderly in
      China
    2. Alleviate loneliness
    3. Have fifty different
      phrases

C. Robot soccer
  1. Mechanical players
  2. Play ice-hockey style
  3. First Robo Cup held
    in Japan, 1997
D. Harvesting robots
  1. Allow California
    farmers to harvest
    crops
  2. Remote laptops used
  3. Save drudgery
E. Military robot (Manny)
  1. Tests clothing for U.S.
    army
  2. Sees how well
    clothing stands up
F. Robot surgeons
  1. Fit into hand
  2. Work inside body
  3. Remove polyps and
    blockages

III. Cloning
  A. Definition
    1. Dolly – cloned lamb
      from adult sheep
    2. Used to produce
      disease-resistant
      herds
  B. Concerns raised
    1. By animal rights
      activists
    2. "Desirable types"
      created

IV. Global warming
  A. What causes it?
    1. CFCs
    2. CO_2
  B. Ozone depletion
    1. Caused by air
      conditioners and
      fridges
    2. Slow turnaround:
      100 years

  C. Effects of technology
    on planet
    1. Damage to crops,
      animals, marine life
    2. Boundaries for
      species shift
    3. Landscape destroyed
    4. Increase in storms
      and climate changes
    5. Nature and humans
      negatively affected

V. Conclusion
  A. Future unfolding now
  B. Some technology
    positive – robots
  C. Some negative – cloning
  D. Long-term effects of
    technology on planet
  E. Need to change
    attitudes about
    technology for future

7. Write the Draft

The purpose of the draft is to write a rough copy of your proposed essay. It is not practical to try to write the final version, yet. Too many changes may still have to be made, because:

- You may change your views on the topic by the end of the writing.

- The body paragraphs may not be in the best order.

- As you work, you may want to add or drop examples. This clarifies the ideas and provides specific support for them.

Save polishing your sentences and wording for the final copy. By doing a draft essay, then revising, editing, and proofreading, you can produce a final copy that is thoughtful, well organized, balanced, coherent, and relatively free of errors.

Introductory Paragraph

Generally, the thesis appears in the first sentence of the introductory paragraph, to give the reader an immediate sense of your perspective on the topic. On occasion, the thesis may not appear until the last sentence of the first paragraph. In a Social Studies essay, for instance, you might start by giving background to an event, to set the stage for your essay and its thesis.

If the essay is three or more pages long, you should have an opening paragraph of at least four to five sentences. The first sentence would likely be the thesis. Sentences 2, 3, and 4 would be about each of the subtopics (assuming you had three).

Although there are a number of new positive technologies available today, other technologies and attitudes toward the environment raise serious concerns about the future. One interesting positive area is the field of robots which will influence housework, pets, recreation, agriculture, the military, and medicine. Cloning, on the other hand, raises serious concerns about the long-term effects. Finally, global warming resulting from increased reliance on technology remains an issue as we enter the new millennium

The last sentence of an introductory paragraph could be a transitional sentence taking the reader into the essay body and the first subtopic. In an introduction, avoid expressions such as "Now I'm going to discuss...," "I will attempt to show you...," or "This essay will explain..." The tone of a formal essay should never be unnecessarily personal or overly obvious.

Body Paragraphs

Each body paragraph should have a topic sentence, and specific evidence that develops the topic sentence. Each time you change topics (or parts, or literary selections, or characters), you should begin a new paragraph. Remember to leave a space before (or indent) each paragraph.

Body paragraphs usually have an idea-example structure to them; that is to say, they present an idea, followed by specific evidence. A paragraph often starts with a topic sentence (an idea) to focus the discussion, followed by an example, followed by a comment on the example, then another example and comment, and so forth.

Robot technology exploded in the 1990s and has already produced such futuristic oddities as personal robots, robot cats, robot soccer, harvesting robots, military robots, and robot surgeons. A two-legged functional robot developed in 1997 in Tokyo walks, finds its way around, and does simple fix-it jobs. So far, its only drawbacks are its limited battery time (fifteen minutes) and cost (hundreds of thousands of dollars). Talking robot cats called Tama were developed in China in 1998, to relieve the loneliness of elderly people living on their own. Tama communicate with their owners and answer simple questions, using a memory bank of fifty different phrases.

Conclusion

Conclusions should never seem to be added on. Typically, the concluding paragraph begins with a sentence connecting it to the topic or thesis. Then it summarizes the main points, referring to the subtopics or sections of the essay. If there are three subtopics, usually there would be a sentence on each one, tying it to the topic. The last sentence (sometimes called the "clincher") should be a memorable overview, leaving the reader with a definite sense of finality — that there is no more to be said on the topic. Concluding paragraphs should always be about the same length as the introduction.

> The future, in a sense, is unfolding *now*. Many of the changes discussed above are already happening and in process. Some technology such as robots is positive and promises to make our lives more leisurely, less arduous, less lonely, and more healthy. Other technologies such as cloning raise far more questions than they solve. In closing, we have taken a more thoughtful overview of what technology is ultimately doing to us and the planet. We need to refocus now; our very survival in the future may depend on it.

Students sometimes wonder why it is not enough to simply repeat or reword the thesis in the clincher. First of all, this would be redundant and might suggest that you had not gone through a process of thinking and developing a response to the topic. Also, by the conclusion, you have explored the topic in some depth, illuminating aspects of it. In other words, you have gone somewhere. What the clincher does is to state where you have arrived, and what final thought you have about the topic.

8. Revise and Edit

Revising and editing occur between the first draft and final copy. Revising generally refers to making larger changes such as in content, while editing focusses more on organization and making corrections.

FOXTROT © 1996 Bill Amend. Reprinted with permission of Universal Press Syndicate. All rights reserved.

After you have written a draft, it is always a good idea to set it aside for a period of time, perhaps an afternoon or a day, and then come back to it to make adjustments and ask questions such as those in the following two charts.

Revising Checklist

Check	Action
Is there evidence for all opinions and views? Is there anything which is false or unprovable? Are there any contradictions?	*Delete any weak ideas or interpretations, and anything that creates ambiguity.*
Can examples be added to make points stronger?	*The most common mistake made is not having enough specific details or evidence.*
Is there a balance of general and specific information?	*Make a tally!*
Are the paragraphs in the best order?	*Re-read your draft after a period of time and you may see a better order of paragraphs.*
Are the paragraphs long enough?	*It is difficult to develop a good paragraph in less than four sentences; the only exception to this would be a transitional paragraph of two to three sentences.*
Are the paragraphs too long?	*Longer than half a page is tough to read and still keep a focus; remember that you should change paragraphs each time you change subtopics, characters, literary selections, or time periods.*
Are the subtopics/sections clearly and logically connected?	*Try to "build more bridges" (that is, use transitional words, phrases, and sentences) between the sections to improve the essay's flow.*
Does each sentence relate to its section, to the topic sentence of its paragraph, and to the thesis in general? Does it add information to the discussion or could it be left out?	*You should delete any sentence which sidetracks, repeats something, presents unhelpful trivia, or contains extraneous, peripheral information.*

Editing Checklist

Check	Action
Are the sentences complete?	*Sentence fragments need to be combined with adjoining sentences. Run-on or comma-spliced sentences should be broken into more than one sentence and punctuated by semicolons or periods.*
Is there enough sentence variety? Could some sentences be combined to form more interesting compound or complex sentences?	*Avoid repeating sentences with subject-verb patterns such as: "He says...; Macbeth knows...; He is..." Remember, if your sentences are monotonous-sounding, the essay will feel boring and predictable to the reader.*
Is the wording clear? Is there any jargon, informal language, or slang?	*If you are unsure about a word or phrase, replace it. Use a dictionary and a thesaurus. Remove jargon, informal language, and slang.*
Are verb tenses consistent throughout?	*Use the present tense (preferred in Language Arts/English essays) or the past tense (preferred in Social Studies/History essays), but not both.*
Does each pronoun have an antecedent word reference?	*Check "he," "she," "they," and "it" to be absolutely clear who each is.*
Does the word "I" appear anywhere?	*An essay is your opinion, so it is unnecessary to periodically write "I think" or "In my opinion."*
Does the word "you" appear anywhere?	*"You" is a word which draws the reader into the essay. A writer cannot presume to tell the reader what the reader thinks, so "you" should not be used.*
Are there any abbreviations?	*Except for words like Ms. or etc., write out words in full.*

9. Proofread

Proofreading refers to the correction of errors in usage, grammar, spelling, punctuation, and capitalization. It is a good idea to have someone else read your revised draft and mark errors, *before* you write a final copy. Often, another pair of eyes can catch things otherwise missed, much in the way that reading a printed hard copy reveals more errors than are picked up when looking at an essay on a computer screen.

If you are keying your essay on a computer, you can use a spell checker, but remember that spell checkers can't sort out homophone choices (words that sound the same, but are spelled differently depending on usage context) or grammar errors. To help you with potential homophone and common usage errors, see the section beginning on p. 126.

If you are a problem speller (that is, you make several spelling errors per page of work), a calculator-sized spell checker is a wise investment. (Sometimes the spell checker is a feature of an electronic dictionary or thesaurus.)

Proofreading Symbols

∧	insert	The house̗ on fire.
ℯ	delete	Rattlesnakes are very v̶e̶r̶y̶ dangerous.
∼	transpose (switch)	Raisa, Louise, and Karin are 12, 14, and 16 years old, respectively.
≡	capital	Planet earth may be in danger.
/	lower case	We Compost all our food scraps.
¶	new paragraph	So that day ended badly. The next day...
⊙	add period	Liu wondered which way to go ⊙
∧̑	add comma	Bring your tent a sleeping bag, and a flashlight.
∨	add apostrophe	"Its Hans!" he cried.
#∧	add space	Daniel and I are leaving tomorrow.
⌣	close space	Chickens can't fly, but ducks can.
....	stet (don't delete)	The pictures are not ready.

Proofreading Checklist

Always read over your work sentence-by-sentence, aloud if possible. If it doesn't sound right, then it probably needs fixing.

- Are all sentences clear and complete?
- Does each verb agree with its subject?
- Does each pronoun agree with its noun reference?
- Is a homophone (e.g., *here, hear*) the right one for the context?
- Are spellings accurate and consistent? (For example, don't switch from *-or* to *-our*, or from *-ise* to *-ize* spellings within the essay.)
- Are all important names and key terms spelled correctly?
- Is there a capital letter at the beginning of each sentence and a period or other end-stop mark at the end of each sentence?
- Have you used a semicolon (;) to punctuate related independent clauses within a sentence?
- Do you want or need all the commas you have used?
- Have you kept exclamation marks to an absolute minimum to register honest surprise or humour?
- Have you kept italics (underlining of words in handwritten work) for emphasis to a minimum?
- Are the initial letters of all names capitalized?
- Are all paragraphs properly spaced or indented?

*What is written
without effort is in general
read without pleasure.*

Samuel Johnson

10. Produce the Final Copy

Just before you write the final copy of your essay, confirm that you know the correct format needed. Usually, teachers will give you specific instructions about how your work is to be presented. If you are unsure about any aspect of format, ask. Below are some things to check out:

- What is the due date?

- How many pages or words are expected?

- Is a title page expected?

Here are a few general guidelines for producing final copy.

Prepare the Final Copy

- Use word processing for your final copy.

- Do not experiment with fonts and design. This is distracting, and can look as though you intended to distract, in order to hide faults in the style or content of your work.

- Print an extra copy (or save on a disk) or make a photocopy of every essay that you submit in case the original is mislaid.

Choose the Paper

- Use letter-size, white, bond paper.

- Print your essay on the best printer that you can access. Use the highest quality setting possible.

Set the Spacing

- Double-space your essay, including quoted materials.

- Set your margins for 2.5 cm (one inch) at the top, bottom, and sides of the text.

- For each new paragraph, indent five spaces, or leave a line space above.

- For block quotations, indent 2.5 cm (one inch).

Choose the Typeface

- For the body of your essay, use a clear legible font between ten and twelve points. You may prefer a different font for titles and headings.

- Align text left.

- Consult the style guide recommended regarding use of italics/underlining.

Set Up the Title

- A title page must include your name, the name of the course, your instructor's name, and the date.

- Instead of a title page, your instructor may direct you to, for example, put this information in the upper left corner and the page number in the upper right. (See page 29.) Check the requirements.

- Centre the title. Do not put the title in quotation marks. If your title is too long to fit on one line, break it into two or more lines.

The Title of the Essay

Your Name

Course and number
Teacher's name
Date submitted

Provide an Outline

- If your instructor requests an outline, give it a separate title page.

Set the Page Numbers

- The first page of your text is page number one. Title pages are not numbered.

- You may want to include your name or initials before the page number (SM9) to identify your essay. Consult a style guide.

- Do not use the abbreviation *p.* before a page number, or add punctuation.

Insert Footnotes

- Footnotes should be double-spaced.

- Quadruple-space between your text and the first footnote at the bottom of the page.

Fastening the Essay

- Fasten the pages with a paper clip. Do not staple it unless your instructor tells you to.

- Use a binder for an essay that is too thick to fasten with a paper clip.

Preparation of Handwritten Essays

Handwritten essays are prepared in a similar way to word-processed essays, with these exceptions.

- Use letter-size, white, ruled paper — looseleaf notebook paper.

- Write on one side only.

- Your instructor may ask you to double-space, that is, write on alternate lines.

- Write in black, blue-black, or blue ink.

- Leave a generous space between words.

- Write as neatly as possible.

- If your handwriting is hard to read, then print your essay.

Final Checklist

Content	See page
• Does your essay need more/better examples and illustrations?	10
• Is the information clear enough for a reader unfamiliar with the subject?	20
• Are there general statements that do not have accompanying details?	20
• Can you show that all your statements are directly related to your topic?	20

Organization

• Is it clear from near the beginning what the essay is about?	13
• Does each paragraph clearly add something to the essay?	20
• Do important statements stand out from less important statements?	13
• Is the order in which you have made important statements logical?	16
• Is the conclusion clear?	18

Diction

• Are there words whose meanings you are not sure of?	21
• Have you used any unfamiliar terms that need explanation?	21
• Is there any unnecessary or awkward repetition?	22
• Are any of your sentences too involved? Do you stumble over some passages as you read your work aloud?	23
• Does the language sound like something you could reasonably be expected to say?	21
• Have you used language (slang or clichés) that is too often heard or read?	21

Grammar and Usage   *See page*

- Have you checked your work specifically   21
  for any errors that you have made in
  previous assignments?

- Have you checked doubtful spellings in a   22
  dictionary?

- Can you justify your punctuation choices?   23

- If a sentence seems confusing, have you   23
  tried to analyse it grammatically for
  structure and punctuation?

Read the Revised and Edited Version

Read over your revised and edited draft one more time before
you go on to write the final copy. Here are some ways you can
do this:

- Read it aloud to yourself or someone else.

- Read it into a tape recorder, replay and listen to it, making
  corrections.

- Have at least one friend or family member (preferably
  someone who is a good speller) read it and make comments.

- Do a quick eye-scan of the essay searching for spelling or other
  obvious errors.

- A recommended proofreading technique is to read over your
  work from the *end* of the essay to the *beginning*, one sentence
  at a time. This method stops the reader from getting caught
  up in meaning rather than paying attention to sentence clarity
  or completeness.

On the following page is a sample of an essay on the future that
has been revised, edited, and proofread. Pay particular
attention to transitions, word choice, punctuation, and the
balance of general and specific information.

SM 1

Sairah Maldon
English 010
Professor Alice Wong
February 11, 2000

The Need to Reconsider Technology in the Future

Although there are a number of new positive technologies available today, other technologies and attitudes toward the environment raise serious concerns about the future. One interesting positive area is the field of robots which will influence housework, pets, recreation, agriculture, the military, and medicine. Cloning, on the other hand, raises serious concerns about the long-term effects. Finally, global warming resulting from increased reliance on technology remains an issue as we enter the new millennium.

Robot technology exploded in the 1990s and has already produced such futuristic oddities as personal robots, robot cats, robot soccer, harvesting robots, military robots, and robot surgeons. A two-legged functional robot developed in 1997 in Tokyo walks, finds its way around, and does simple fix-it jobs. So far, its only drawbacks are its limited battery time (fifteen minutes) and cost (hundreds of thousands of dollars). "Talking" robot cats called Tama were developed in China in 1998 to relieve the loneliness of elderly people living on their own. Tama communicate with their owners and answer simple questions, using a memory bank of fifty different phrases.

Recreationally, robot soccer consists of miniature mechanical players who kick, run, pass a ball, and play in teams. They are controlled by remote radio links and are developed enough to have played in the First Robo Cup held in Japan in 1997. In the area of agriculture, unmanned robot machines are used to harvest crops automatically by farmers with laptops! This agricultural revolution has removed repetitive and tedious farm work.

On another practical note, in the American military, a two-million-dollar robot called Manny is used to test the durability of military clothing for the army. In medicine, hand-sized robot surgeons called endobots have been developed to perform surgery inside the human body. These are less than one millimetre square and might be inserted into the ear or even swallowed. The endobot itself consists of a computer, sensors, antennae, and a claw for lifting. This device will be used to remove blockages and polyps, starting in the first decade of the new millennium.

A less obvious necessary and certainly more controversial technology is cloning, a complex process to duplicate species. In 1997, Scottish researchers cloned Dolly, a lamb which was a genetic duplicate of an adult sheep. Although Dolly was seen as a breakthrough to dramatically improve livestock, more concerns have since focussed on possible misuses rather than the benefits of this development.

Animal rights activists, for instance, protest treating experimental animals as unfeeling objects. More serious, though, is the fear that cloning might be used to create human life. Given that cloning could lead to such bizarre possibilities as alternate versions of oneself, and the creation of certain "desirable" types, it is clear that cloning has the potential to be a dangerous technology.

What started as an innocent, helpful breakthrough in agriculture is now being addressed by governments around the world in anti-cloning legislation. The old saying comes to mind — just because something can be done, doesn't necessarily mean it is natural, morally right, or free from controversy and debate.

As technology comes to dominate the fabric of early millennium life, it continues to be obvious that the ecology of the planet is in jeopardy. Nowhere is this more evident than in the ozone layer depletion problem.

CFC emissions rise and the presence of CO_2 has now doubled in the atmosphere. As well, fossil fuels burned by cars, factories, and power plants continue to increase the number of warm gases and air pollutants. Since the discovery of the ozone hole over Antarctica and the thinning ozone layer over the Arctic, earth-based monitoring systems reveal that the earth is getting warmer because of increased use and spread of technology.

Despite some legislation changes and important environment conferences, the turnaround is very slow and optimistically estimated at 100 years! In the meantime, the environment bears the tragic imprint of global warming. In Canada, boundaries for vegetation and wildlife shift north. In the North, roads and airstrips are destroyed by permafrost melt. The number of severe storms and disruption in climate patterns put crops, animals, fish spawning grounds, and wetlands all in peril.

Because of harmful radiation which is left unchecked, human beings are experiencing increases in the instances of skin cancer, eye cataracts, and weakened immune systems. The message continues to be clear as we overconsume, thoughtlessly use air conditioners and refrigerators, and don't press our politicians for environmental upgrading: if we don't become more responsible with our technology and change our attitude toward the planet, then we could well destroy it and ourselves.

The future, in a sense, is unfolding now. Many of the changes discussed above are already happening and in process. Some technology such as robots is positive and promises to make our lives more leisurely, less arduous, less lonely, and more healthy. Other technologies such as cloning raise far more questions than they solve. In closing, we have to take a more thoughtful overview of what technology is ultimately doing to us and the planet. We need to refocus now; our very survival in the future may depend on it.

Part 2

Specific Forms of Writing and Representing

Writing about Literature

Most of the essays that you will write in high school will be for English assignments. Most of these essays will be about literature, as will any that you write for English at the college or university level.

Standard Features of Essays about Literature

In writing essays about literature (that is, literary criticism) you must:

Interact with the literature.

- Think carefully about what you have read, and have reasonable critical responses as you discuss the literature in relation to the given topic.

- You will have to suspend judgment, initially, and read the work on its own terms, looking for patterns and purpose.

Analyse the literature.

- Examine ideas and themes, characters and their motivation, and their choices, causes and effects, symbols and their meanings.

- Go beyond the literal level to discuss the figurative level.

Avoid giving a plot summary.

Assume the person reading your essay has already read the selection. What he or she is interested in are things like:

- Do you understand what you have read? Can you distinguish between the literal and figurative levels of meaning?

- Can you perceive what is important about the work even if it is not directly stated? That is, can you read between the lines, or below the surface?

- Can you respond to the selection in a mature, reasonable, thoughtful, and sensitive way?

- Can you appreciate the form (the techniques and style) of the work?

Be specific.

- A common mistake in essay writing is to be too general. Specific examples are needed to show that you know how to back up an interpretation or opinion.

- Using specific examples demonstrates that you have read the text, and know it well.

Be accurate.

- Fuzzy notions won't work in a literary criticism. You have to be very clear about what you want to say.

- Your facts have to be accurate. Every time you mention a character or event, that information cannot be false — otherwise you have committed a basic error. Referring to a character by a wrong name or misspelling a character's name are inexcusable factual errors.

Use the correct term.

hero	a character looked up to by the reader and other characters
protagonist	the main character in a work
moral	a lesson of the selection
theme	the main idea of the selection
narrator	the character or person who tells a fictional narrative such as a short story, novel, or play
speaker	someone speaking lines of poetry or dialogue

Refer to a selection by its genre.

Don't call a play, movie, or novel "a story." The only time you should use "story" is to refer to a short story. If by "story," you mean the narrative of a work, then use the concise term "plot."

Use relevant literary terms.

Using terms appropriately will help to communicate your understandings of the literature, as well as show that you are familiar with and have mastered literary terms and related concepts.

- If you are writing an essay about character, use character-related terms such as:

epiphany	a moment of intense realization for the protagonist
foil	a character who brings out the features of the protagonist, by contrast
goal	the protagonist's objective
motivation	the reason the character does what he or she does

- If you are analysing a poem, mention relevant techniques such as the following:

image	a physical description that affects the reader's senses:
	Life is a broken-winged bird that cannot fly.
metaphor	a direct comparison that states one thing is symbolically the same as another:
	When it comes to running, she's a deer.
personification	the assigning of human qualities to non-human things:
	Pale sunlight tiptoed through the clouds.
simile	a comparison that implies one thing is like another, using *like* or *as*:
	She ran like a deer or *She ran as fast as a deer.*
symbol	an object that represents something else:
	The maple leaf is a symbol of Canada.

Use some quotations.

In each literary selection, there are memorable or important lines that encapsulate author views, character attitudes, conflicts, and themes.

- Using three to five good, key quotations from a selection in a prepared essay shows that you have read the text closely and understand what is important.

- It is important to set up the quotation, to indicate how it illustrates a point.

- Short quotations (one sentence or less) should be worked into sentences with a minimum of disruption to the flow of the essay. The quotation should be smoothly integrated with the text and should be commented on:

> Romeo reveals his desire and impatience when he says, "O, wilt thou leave me so unsatisfied?" This rash comment is typical of the haste that will later lead to his sudden, impetuous choice of suicide.

- Longer quotations should be indented and keyed double-spaced. Page numbers (for fiction or essays) or line numbers (for poetry or verse drama) should be given. For example, in an essay on Robert Frost's "Stopping by Woods on a Snowy Evening," you might quote a stanza to focus a discussion on some aspect of the poem:

> The last stanza suggests the seductiveness of the woods — of "dropping out" of human society:
>
> > The woods are lovely, dark, and deep,
> >
> > But I have promises to keep,
> >
> > And miles to go before I sleep,
> >
> > And miles to go before I sleep. (13-16)
>
> However, the poet is aware of promises he has made — responsibilities and social obligations — which necessitate his leaving the woods.

- Generally speaking, it is better to keep quotations to five or fewer (in an essay of four or five pages) and most of these should be short, that is, easy to read. Using too many quotations is like letting someone else do your work for you.

Common Literary Perspectives and Themes

Since literature is predictably about life and human nature, certain perspectives recur. These include the following views:

- **Purpose is the most important aspect of any literary work.**
  Ask yourself why the author wrote the work. What did he or she want to say about a given subject, life in general, or human nature? An author may have a very serious purpose, perhaps related to theme: in *Lord of the Flies* one theme is that humankind has survived despite its tendency toward violence, war, and destruction. Relevant to this, one of William Golding's purposes is to show us the darkness of the human heart.

- **Most protagonists have to make significant life-altering choices.**
  Such choices are based on the character's beliefs and values as well as the situation and limiting circumstances. Some choices will turn out to be positive or life-enhancing, culminating in personal growth, positive change, and increased happiness or perspective. Other choices, especially in tragedy, will be negative and destructive because of character flaws — the result is death, disaster, or hardship for the protagonist and other characters.

- **There will always be a number of conflicts.**
  Much literature isn't about very obvious physical conflicts like shootouts or car chases. Instead, conflicts will be between characters with differing attitudes, or within the mind of a single character. These conflicts will typically be emotional, mental, and spiritual in nature.

- **Most selections will present a dual view of human experience.**
  Popular pairs of topics include: good and evil, reality and illusion, conformity and rebellion, the individual and society, tradition and change, love and betrayal, materialism and spirituality. In works like *Macbeth, The Mosquito Coast, Lord of the Flies,* and *Hamlet,* authors reveal the dual nature of human beings: characters can have contradictory sides that lead to opposing values and beliefs.

- **Most selections contain irony.**
  Because human beings behave in contradictory ways, and there is more than one view of just about any situation, many selections are ironic. People often turn out to be different from what they first appear to be, the truth of a situation may be different from its appearance, and situations may turn out differently from what was expected. For both reader and protagonist, there is often a learning aspect to ironic misjudgments, errors, and any resulting suffering.

When you don't read,
you don't write.

Helen Barolini

Following is an example of an essay on a famous movie often studied as text in mythology units. As you are reading it, take note of some of the points just discussed and how they are used to advantage in this essay.

Heroes in <u>Star Wars</u>

Princess Leia, Obi-Wan Kenobi, and Luke Skywalker are three examples of heroes in the George Lucas movie <u>Star Wars</u>. Leia's purpose is to help her people and she is able to achieve this mainly by motivating others to fight with the Rebels. Obi-Wan is a Jedi knight who teaches Luke the mysterious ways of the Force. Luke takes Obi-Wan's teachings and puts them into practice by destroying the Death Star. All these heroes are committed to a significant goal and put others ahead of themselves as they fight the Dark Side.

   Princess Leia is determined to protect her home planet against the evil Empire. Although she finds herself in many precarious situations, she is never at all concerned about herself. During interrogation, for instance, she stands up fearlessly to Darth Vader and Grand Moft Tarkin, refusing to give them any information which might endanger Alderon. Later, she tells Han that "somebody has to save us kids" and pushes them into the garbage compactor. It is also worth remembering that she is the one who suggests they brace the moving bin walls. Looking out for others is second nature for Princess Leia.

   Obi-Wan Kenobi is another selfless hero who acts as Luke's protector and advisor. He saves Luke from the Sand People's attack and begins to teach Luke the instinctive ways of using a light-sabre and following the Force. His superior knowledge and special skills are shown in the scenes when he uses telepathy to frustrate the police on the outpost streets and his light-sabre on the monsters in the airport bar. He is also the one who shuts down the Death Star's power/tractor beam and acts as a decoy, sacrificing his life in a duel with Vader so the others might escape. However, Obi-Wan's spirit and wisdom live on in the character of Luke Skywalker.

The last time they see one another, Obi-Wan says, "Your destiny lies along a different path from mine."

In the beginning of the movie, Luke is an adolescent orphan whose goals are to avenge the deaths of his aunt and uncle, and to find the princess recorded by R2-D2. He follows the message's lure and ends up enduring many trials on her behalf, rescuing her on the Death Star and becoming the lone pilot who ultimately destroys the Star. It is necessary in the process that Luke dies to his child-self while assuming the responsibilities of adulthood. This is accomplished when he instinctively heeds the words of his mentor Obi-Wan to "use the Force."

Princess Leia, Obi-Wan Kenobi, and Luke Skywalker portray several heroic characteristics and attitudes. Leia's example gives life and inspiration to her followers. Obi-Wan uses the Force to instruct others and enhance their possibilities. Luke embodies the teachings of his elder god-teacher and puts them into successful practice for a higher purpose. All three heroes are strong, brave, and have positive moral impact on their world in the movie Star Wars.

Work Cited
Star Wars (A New Hope). Dir. George Lucas. Twentieth Century Fox, 1977.

Exam Essays about Literature

In this common type of essay, there is automatically a time restriction. The writer has to present what was discussed in "Writing about Literature," but has to do it without much time to plan, organize, revise, edit, and proofread. There is no second chance, no extra time. The writer has to be pre-prepared, focussed, quick to organize, and thoughtful. This essay type presents a variety of difficulties which call for prompt solutions. Below are some suggestions for dealing with the extra stress of writing an essay under pressure:

Problem	*Solution*
• *On an exam, you have to read some literature which you have not seen before, and interpret it.*	• Read the selection carefully; read any footnotes on vocabulary or allusions provided.
	• Use a dictionary to check any unfamiliar words.
	• Underline important words, phrases, or lines; if some words present an alternate point of view, then circle those, to see the conflict better.
	• Try to boil down the selection to a familiar theme or conflict; make a diagram of both sides of the conflict, using words from the selection.
	• Mention and quote details from the selection to back up what you are writing.
	• Relate the selection to any topic or instructions given.
	• It is helpful to look for patterns (such as conflicts) and overall structure — to examine images, word choice, *mood* (created in the reader), *tone* (attitude of the author toward the subject or situation).
• *You have to give a personal response.*	• This means that you can use examples from your personal experience; if you have not personally had a relevant experience, you can mention your observations about the experiences of those closest to you, such as family and friends.

- You might refer to a famous quotation, or a relevant book or movie that addresses the topic.
- You should show yourself to be thoughtful and mature.

You don't have enough time to plan during an exam.

- Study well in advance: anticipate topics, review old essays, go over literature, check spellings of characters' and authors' names.
- Block some time for planning and stick to your self-imposed time limit — if you are writing an eighty-minute essay, take at least ten to fifteen minutes to plan; for a three-hour exam, twenty to thirty minutes planning and organizing would not be unreasonable. *You may not have time to do a draft, so good planning and a rough outline are the main keys.*
- The most important thing is to have a plan and an order that makes sense *before* you start writing.
- If you are analysing a topic about a character or one work of literature, a chronological order tracing the character's development or the development of a theme, conflict, or symbol in the selection works well. Take care not to simply summarize the plot.

You're not sure which literature to use.

- Pick the *best* works you know that fit the topic.
- Don't use any literature which feels "light"; use obvious or strong literature, preferably major works such as novels, plays, or films.
- You should be able to use many examples and even quote from the literature you pick.
- In many cases, it's best to use literature you are most familiar with.

• *You're not sure what to put in the introduction.*	• You must mention the topic and give your thesis. • Say which literature or characters you are using, in the order of their appearance in the body paragraphs. • Your introduction should be four to five sentences; one approach is to have a statement about the topic for the first sentence, then one sentence on each of the various subtopics, followed by the thesis.
• *You have to analyse under pressure.*	• It helps to have studied and to know the literature well *before* you walk into the exam room. This means you should be able to give many details and about three key quotes from the literary work(s). • Don't panic and start telling the plot without analysis; keep referring to the topic and moving back and forth between general and specific levels.
• *You're not sure what to put in the conclusion.*	• Your first sentence should refer to the topic and/or thesis. Then you should review the findings of your essay, summarizing the main points. Follow this with the "clincher" — a logical conclusion or judgment about the topic and its significance. • The "clincher" should sound final and be memorable for the reader.
• *You have to be clear and x*	• When finished, read over the essay sentence-by-sentence — if a sentence sounds awkward, recast it. Make sure all sentences are complete and can stand alone. • Make sure verb tenses are consistent, and that all pronouns have clear antecedent references. • Check the context for any homophones to be sure you've spelled them correctly.

- Check spellings using the dictionary, thesaurus, or a spell checker. Characters' and authors' names should be carefully spelled.
- Review any apostrophes you've used — are they needed and are they placed correctly?
- If you have time, add brief transitions — e.g., "in fact," "therefore."
- Replace any weak wording — e.g., "interesting," "good," "sad" — using your thesaurus.
- Edit out anything that is repetitious, contradictory, or irrelevant.
- It is *very* important that you leave yourself time to read over your work before you turn it in; try to leave yourself a *minimum* of 10 minutes to do this.

- *You need to add or delete information at the last moment.*

- Add information using numbered footnotes; put the extra information on the blank facing page of exam booklets, at the bottom of the page, in the margins, or on the reverse side of the page if it's blank.
- Delete words or phrases *neatly* using liquid paper; for longer sections, use brackets, x's, and/or cross out lines, and write "delete."

Writing comes more easily if you have something to say.

Sholem Asch

Following is an example of an exam essay.

Good and Evil in Lord of the Flies

William Golding's novel Lord of the Flies is a classic illustration of the conflict between good and evil and a significant allegory on the human condition. The plot concerns a group of young English schoolboys marooned on an unidentified desert island without any adult survivors. At first, they try to set up a microcosm of the civilized adult society they left behind them in England. Decent characters such as Ralph and the intellectual Piggy become the natural guardians organizing this new society. However, a countergroup is established by Jack who distracts the boys into "fun and games" which, in turn, leads to killing pigs and, eventually, killing humans. Life on the island moves quickly from good intentions to evil results, revealing what Golding calls "the heart of man's darkness."

The young survivors of the plane crash have been affected by their civilized society with a sense of rules and order. With the best intentions, they set up a version of democracy, recalling the ancient Greek system, complete with "speaker staff" – the conch – which is also used to summon the boys to the first assembly. There is a roll call to identify survivors; then Ralph is chosen as chief. He insists on rules and organizational procedures to be followed and is supported by Piggy, his counsellor, who gives a "grown-up" air to the start-up of this new society.

At first, things go reasonably well with the hut-building for shelter and the long-range plan to maintain a signal fire, but there is a foreshadowing of chaos and the evil to come when the boys accidentally burn down half the island and some of the boys are killed by the fire. "Fun and games" gives way to the hunters enthusiastically killing pigs and smearing their faces with war paint that symbolizes their increasing regression to savagery.

The boys also become increasingly superstitious and instinctively run from the dead pilot on the mountain, thinking he is the Beast from Air. Golding shows that fear and imagination lead naturally to primitive superstition culminating in the scene with the pig's head on a stick, a symbol of evil and an allusion to "Lord of the Flies," another name for Beelzebub or the Devil.

Gradually, responsibilities are neglected, quarrels increase, calls to assembly are ignored, hut-building is abandoned, and a chance to be rescued is missed because someone lets the fire go, symbolically, out. A split in the ranks finally happens when Jack chooses to go off to become a full-time hunter, setting up his own primitive society.

The good characters become fewer. Simon, who knows the truth about the pilot, is ruthlessly murdered, and even the last two good characters – Piggy and Ralph – take part in the frenzied ritualistic killing of Simon. At this point, Jack and evil have gained the upper hand. Jack's one-man tyranny, his fascistic "might is right" mentality, and the open disdain and hostility toward Ralph and Piggy dominate life on the island.

The next major turning point is the sadistic murder of Piggy, which signifies the death of reason (foreshadowed earlier by the smashing and theft of his glasses). Good, reason, and life give way to evil, instinct, fear, and death. Co-operation, trust, friendship, loyalty, peace, and order degenerate into selfishness, suspicion, hate, violence and, ultimately, chaos and war. Ralph, the lone survivor representing good, is hunted like a pig and it looks, in the last chapter, as if evil has won the day.

But just as Ralph is "smoked out" onto the beach, he is surprisingly rescued by the Navy commander. Golding seems to be saying that human beings have survived thus far in spite of themselves and their barbaric nature, and that civilization may only be superficially schoolboy-uniform-deep. The reader is left wondering how "saved" Ralph really is since the commander is a reminder of war and destruction – a macrocosm of what the boys have been playing at on their microcosm paradise-turned-dystopia – and that that macrocosm is what the boys are returning to at the end of the book.

Lord of the Flies continues to shock and be truthful at the same time for a new generation of readers. It shows, on one hand, the best longings of human beings – the desire for a utopian ideal. Conversely, it also shows the all-too-real, defective sides of human nature that threaten our very existence on the planet. William Golding's pessimistic Lord of the Flies remains a fascinating study of the ongoing struggle between good and evil.

Writing a Character Sketch

The task of writing a character sketch is best completed through planning similar to the following.

For a character sketch in essay form, you might begin by dividing your page in two. Label the left side *Character Trait* and label the right side *Evidence*. On the left side, list the adjectives that describe the personality of the character. On the right, list the specific detail that supports your observation. Your evidence can be based on one or more of the following:

- what the character says
- what the character thinks
- what the character does
- what the author, or the other characters, say about the character
- how others react to the character.

The above evidence, direct or indirect, will provide strong support for each character trait you identify.

Once you have identified a number of words describing the personality of the character, link related words that could be discussed in the same paragraph. Then, begin to write. Comment on the related words to show their significance to the literary work.

Following is an example of an extended character sketch done for the protagonist of Shakespeare's *King Lear*.

Lear as Dynamic Character

In *King Lear*, Shakespeare presents a central figure whose character is the author of his own demise. King Lear, a powerful and autocratic king at the start of the play, loses his family, friends, and power, but ends up a simple, appreciative, and humane individual. It is Lear's character that brings about his own downfall and the deaths of his daughters.

At the beginning of the play, Lear is an arrogant, self-centred, and temperamental ruler. He impulsively decides that he wants to divide his kingdom among his three daughters so that he can "unburthen'd crawl toward death" (1.1.41). The three daughters speak, from the eldest (Goneril) to the second youngest (Regan) to the youngest (Cordelia). Goneril and Regan falsely praise Lear, telling him that they love him more than anything in the world. Cordelia has trouble being anything but sincere, and tells Lear that she has nothing to say. When he prompts her, she explains that she loves him "according to my bond, no more nor less" (1.1.93). Lear mistakes her sincerity for failure to say how much she loves him; then he ruthlessly disinherits and banishes her.

Once the kingdom has been divided between the two elder daughters, King Lear decides to go to stay with Goneril. Within a short time, Goneril is unhappy that Lear's soldiers are setting up house in her castle. She tells Lear she wants him to cut his train in half. Lear objects and decides to leave Goneril to go to Regan, whom he hopes will accept all his men. At Gloucester's castle on the way to Regan's, he discovers how much Kent has been mistreated by Regan and her husband. From these events, we learn more about Lear's character. He is easily outraged and his temper is more than evident. As well, he is frustrated because Regan is turning out to be more in favour of Goneril than of him. When he rages against Regan and decides to head out into the wilderness during a horrible storm, we see how Lear's temper gets the best of him, and we learn that he now is feeling remorse over his treatment of Cordelia.

Out in the storm, Lear rants and then settles down as he realizes the Fool has no shelter from the storm:

> My wits begin to turn.
> Come on, my boy. How dost, my boy? Art cold?
> I am cold myself. Where is this straw, my fellow?
> The art of our necessities is strange,
> And can make vile things precious. Come, your hovel,
> Poor Fool and knave, I have one part in my heart
> That's sorry yet for thee. (3.2.67-73)

This acknowledgment of the Fool's suffering is new for Lear, who previously was so self-centred that he could not also consider Cordelia's feelings.

The time spent in the storm challenges and weakens Lear. A man who used to be a king, dressed in finery, and sleeping in the most comfortable of quarters has suddenly been turned outdoors, and left with no luxuries. He is humbled by his predicament, and the feelings he expresses for the Fool's comfort are a sign that Lear is becoming less self-centred and more aware of the suffering of others. Again, such a realization makes him aware of the depth of the wrong he did to Cordelia.

Lear gradually loses his senses and rails against his daughters. In the hovel with Edgar and the Fool, Lear is overwhelmed by the ingratitude of his children and angrily proceeds to put them on mock trial. Eventually, his lunatic ravings are interrupted by Gloucester, who warns him to get away quickly to join Cordelia at Dover. Again, Lear learns how very wrong his decision to divide his kingdom was, for now Goneril and Regan are not only seeking his death, but they are also secretly competing with each other for land and to gain the attentions of Edgar. This greed on the part of the daughters simply underscores how short-sighted Lear was when he originally divided the kingdom.

In the end, Lear is reduced from the arrogant, temperamental, self serving king to a humble old man who is considerate of others and who has self-knowledge: "I am a very foolish fond old man . . . I fear I am not in my perfect mind" (4.7.59-62). And later, he says, "Pray you now, forget and forgive. I am old and foolish" (4.7.84). As these quotations illustrate, Lear has become more modest and is no longer the raging, arrogant king that he once was. He begs forgiveness from Cordelia and looks forward to their reunited future together. Finally, the unnecessary murder of Cordelia breaks his heart and spirit, and he dies pathetically — mad and isolated.

At the start of the play King Lear is a conceited, self-centred, proud man who is caught up with dividing his kingdom and in giving himself a break from the duties of kingship. We see him go from being ungrateful and temperamental to being greatly humbled and loving, and finally despairing — a broken man who realizes too late the errors of his poor choice. For this reason, the sense of tragedy is stronger because of the profound character change in Lear. We sense that he was capable of greatness and that his death is genuinely tragic.

Writing a Live Play Review

The intention of a review is to discuss the purpose and main ideas of the work, giving details to support your views. Good reviews usually mention techniques as well as the subject matter. Often, both positive and negative features are mentioned, in all but really good or very weak dramas.

Begin by considering your audience — Who are they? What will they expect from a review? Next, consider what you have to say and organize your points and examples. Here is a typical outline for a review of a live play:

Introduction

List the basic information: title, director, main actors, theatre, and running dates.

Paragraph 1

Give a general overview of the story line, without giving away the ending. Briefly comment on the relevance of the plot, or mention theme/purpose.

Paragraph 2

Comment on the main actors' performances — who was the strongest actor, who did a good job, and who was miscast.

Paragraph 3

Comment on technical aspects such as sets, staging, lighting, sound, music, art direction.

Conclusion

Conclude by drawing some observations about the success of the play and about the acting. Was the production good? What were its strengths? What were its weaknesses? How would most people react to it? Was the drama's purpose fulfilled? Then pass judgment on the direction, and the drama's success, fulfilment of purpose, impact, or meaningfulness.

Following is an example of a play review.

Salesman Great Season Opener for Playhouse

director: Janice Welles

stars: Hugh Edwards
   Lynn Tucker
   James O'Neil
   Allan Sutherland

theatre: The Playhouse

dates: Sept. 17-30

Arthur Miller's play *Death of a Salesman* is an oft-revived staple of American theatre. Willy Loman is the unlikely tragic hero who feels "kind of temporary" about himself. His inability to resolve his own conflicts is mirrored in the paralysed development of his two sons Biff and Happy. Miller's play is a powerful reminder of the dangers of the materialistic American dream and Janice Welles' production effectively captures Willy's fall and his sons' redemption.

In any production of *Salesman*, much depends on the casting of the Loman family and Welles' choices are inspired. As Willy, Hugh Edwards has just the right amount of world-weariness which he conveys from the moment he first enters with his two suitcases. He gives us a many-faceted characterization from the authoritarian father to the philanderer to the braggart. He is matched by Lynn Tucker who plays a convincingly loyal Linda who keeps her man's hopes up for most of the play. Tucker is strongest in the scene where she insists that Willy not "be allowed to fall into his grave like an old dog."

James O'Neil makes a suitably angry young Biff who goes head-to-head with his father in the "dime a dozen" showdown speech in Act 2. He is counterpointed by a smart-alecky Happy, played by Allan Sutherland in his first Playhouse appearance. Together, these two embody the conflicts that their father cannot resolve — the dreams of peddler and pioneer.

Shauna Hussain has rendered a subtle, dreamlike set complete with the windowless, doorless façade of a two-storey house in Brooklyn. Paul Sharma's back-curtain lighting creates the illusion of autumn leaves and urban claustrophobia boxing in the Lomans and their house. Only the recorded flute music seemed a little too obvious. Surely, there are enough good local musicians to give voice to Willy's theme and longings!

Overall, though, this is a fine, sensitive *Salesman*. Welles gets strong, memorable performances from this competent cast and blows life into this classic favourite. If you are in the mood for a thoughtful night at the theatre, then this production should not be missed.

Writing Poetry

Poetry takes many forms: a highly structured sonnet, free verse, a simple two-line couplet, and so on. You may want your poem to tell a story, express an emotion, describe a scene, or simply play with words. Most poems are intended to evoke some kind of emotional reaction in the audience, and to achieve that purpose in the most intense, compact, and efficient way possible.

What all poetic forms have in common is the way in which the language is used — it is often more vivid and intense than the language of prose or everyday speech. You can achieve this intensity in all sorts of ways: through imagery, rhythm (metre), rhyme, word sounds, allusions, even punctuation and the way the poem is set on the page.

Imagery

You can use figurative language, such as similes and metaphors (see page 37), to express your feelings in a concentrated way.

Rhythm

Metre is the rhythm of the stressed and unstressed syllables of a poem read aloud. Choose your metre to reflect the mood of your poem.

Rhyme

Some poems rhyme; others don't. Poems that rhyme usually have a regular rhyming pattern, such as *abab*, in which the first and third lines sometimes rhyme, and the second and fourth lines rhyme.

Word Sounds: Onomatopoeia and Alliteration

Writers, especially poets, often choose words for the way they sound as well as for their meaning — it adds another dimension to the writing. **Onomatopoeic words** are words that imitate actual sounds: *hiss*, *thud*, *crash*, *hush*, and *twitter*. **Alliteration** is the repetition of the same consonant sound at the beginnings of successive words: *Round and round the rugged rocks he ran.*

Allusion

An allusion is a brief reference to something from history, literature, or culture as a way of adding meaning to your writing. For example, you may allude to Helen of Troy as a way of describing a fascinating woman. A reader who recognizes the allusion will have an image of the legendary Helen, and you have no need to elaborate.

Punctuation and Layout

Poems are often arranged in verses. Verses may consist of an equal number of lines, or they may vary in length. Consider starting a new verse when the topic or point of view is changing, just as you would begin a new paragraph of an essay.

Poetry doesn't usually follow the rules of punctuation that apply to prose. Because most poems are meant to be read aloud, you may use line breaks and punctuation to create rhythm, or to show where the reader should pause.

Breaking lines in order to form shapes on the page is another way that poets play with the rules. See page 60 for an example of this.

Writing a Free-Verse Poem

Free verse is the most common type of poetry written in the past hundred years by serious poets. It has no regular rhyme or rhythm and depends on images, spacing, and punctuation for its effects. Below are suggestions for a way of writing a free-verse poem.

Brainstorm ideas to write about.

The first challenge in writing a free-verse poem is to choose something to write about.

In this example, the task is to recall a memory of a time before you started school, and to write about that memory. List the memories that you have to choose from:

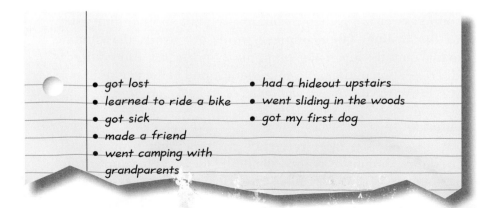

- got lost
- learned to ride a bike
- got sick
- made a friend
- went camping with grandparents
- had a hideout upstairs
- went sliding in the woods
- got my first dog

Get ready to write.

The next step is to draw a picture of the memory, to help you focus on details. Then write a list of words describing the memory, in phrases one under the other:

image list:
- new sled for Christmas
- cold out
- see my breath
- snow squeaks
- position sled at top of hill
- hop on board and coast down hill
- ride is bumpy
- wolves out at bottom of hill
- I fall off the sled and go rolling
- wolves start to run toward me
- I gather up the sled and run up the hill before the wolves can get me

Write the draft.

Write down specific, concrete words or phrases describing the memory. Then organize them into coherent phrases or sentences. Create stanzas if necessary. Check the ending for finality. Think of a suitable title.

Sliding Hill
The winter wind seeps
through my parka's thick folds
and stings my ears numb

My breath blows steamy clouds
of whiteness
into the still night air
and the packed snow squeaks
beneath my boots' hard soles

At the top of the sliding hill
I place my new wooden sled
climb on board
and sail slowly
         faster
            faster yet
until
I'm in the air
  falling
    rolling
      sprawling

Then, the sled disappears into darkness
and the wolves
under shadowy pines
rise on silent paws
        stretch
and run toward me

Tips for revising the poem

- Make sure you are writing in the present tense.

- Try to end with the strongest thought or image.

- Space lines inward from the left margin as well as downward.

- Divide lines for effect in units that can be read in one sweep of the eyes.

- Avoid clichés—e.g., fluffy clouds, pretty flowers

Writing a Short Story

A short story is a piece of fiction that involves conflict and resolution. Short stories can be as short as half a page, although most are longer than that. Because of the length restrictions they face, writers of short stories must make every sentence count.

Elements in a Short Story

Plot

What happens in the story? Is it believable? Does the action move quickly enough? Does it come to a satisfying and logical conclusion?

Character

Characters are revealed mainly through what they say and do, what others say about them, and how others react to them. Other elements can also contribute to creating a believable character: physical appearance, belongings, habits or characteristics, and ways of talking.

Setting

The setting — where the story takes place — is the backdrop for the plot, but it can also contribute to the theme, the mood, and even the characters in a story. A story set in a graveyard at midnight, for example, already raises the reader's expectations regarding what might happen, and sets a definite mood.

Conflict

The conflict in a short story arises out of the characters and the situation. The main character may be in conflict with another character; with him- or herself; or with some outside force, such as nature (for example, a character may be struggling to survive during a flood or other disaster).

Theme

The theme of a story is the overall message about human nature or life that you want to convey. Not directly stated, it is expressed through all the elements of the story: the plot, the characters, the setting, the conflict, and the symbols.

Mood

The mood of a story is the feeling or attitude that it expresses (for example, sad, cheerful, dark, thoughtful, menacing). Writers establish mood through the words they choose, their descriptions of characters, and through the setting of the story.

Point of View

You can write from many different points of view. Your narrator may be a character in the story itself, writing in the first person (I, me). Other stories are written from the point of view of one of the characters, but using the third person (he, she, they, it). Still other stories have an outside narrator who knows everything, and who can tell the reader what any character is thinking or doing at any time. This omniscient (all-seeing) narrator can report what is happening in two different places at the same time, and can compare the thoughts of different characters to the same events.

Writing Your Story

There are several ways to start a story. One common method is to create a character, and develop a story around this character. Below is a process that can help you develop a story from memory and via characterization:

Write a memory of a specific instance.
Examples:

- the smell of newly mown grass

- the sound of a heavy rainfall

- the sight of a newborn pony

- the feel of warm beach sand

- the taste of ice cream

> *You can't wait for inspiration.*
> *You have to go after it with a club.*
>
> Jack London

Find a magazine photograph of the featured character.
Cut the photograph out and tape it to a blank sheet of paper.

Answer a series of questions about the character.
Sample questions:

- What is your character's name? How old is he or she?
- Where does your character live?
- How far did the character go in school? What kind of student was the character?
- What are his or her most important possessions?
- Does the character work? If so, where?
- What does the character fear most?
- Does the character believe in a particular religion or philosophy?
- What does he or she want most from life?
- What is an immediate problem the character is facing?
- What are his or her favourite sports?
- Who are the character's best friends?

Write a brief biography for the character, giving the memory you chose to the character.
Rewrite the memory in the third person. Change the memory to make it fit the character.

Read the third-person memory to a small group.
Then ask the group to help you to find a conflict you could focus on.

Revise the third person memory to bring out the conflict.
Continue the memory until you have a fully developed story.

Organize the sequence of events.
Short stories are organized according to time sequence. You may begin at any point in the sequence of events. Events that happened before the story begins can be explained as the story unfolds: by flashbacks, from what the characters say, or from explanations provided by the narrator.

Take your story through a revising and editing process.
Read your final draft to the class.

Writing a Script

A script is the written text of a play, movie, radio or television show, or other dramatic presentation. As well as dialogue (spoken words), you must write directions that tell what actions, sounds, images, or events should take place as the words are being spoken.

Elements in a Script

A dramatic script has much the same elements as a short story — plot, character, setting, conflict, theme, mood, and point of view. The beginning introduces the characters and the setting, and sets up the situation or conflict. The middle of the script tells what happens when the conflict gets worse (the *climax*). The end shows how the conflict is resolved.

A script is divided into scenes. Just as every paragraph in an essay has to relate back to the main idea, so every scene in a play must have a purpose: to develop a character, set the mood, or move the plot along. Whenever the setting, the time, or the point of view changes, a new scene begins.

Scripts share all the main features of short stories. However, where a short story relies heavily on the narrator to provide information about the thoughts and feelings of the characters, scriptwriters have to rely largely on dialogue and action. To help compensate for these limitations, scripts — especially plays — use certain conventions that are not found in other forms of fiction.

Script Conventions

Monologue

A monologue (a long, uninterrupted speech by one actor) can be used as a way of focussing the audience's attention on one character's thoughts or experiences. It is also a good way to introduce background information about the character or plot. However, too many monologues will slow down the pace of your script and make it sound artificial.

Soliloquy

A soliloquy (a speech made by one character to himself or herself, or directly to the audience) can be used to reveal a character's inner thoughts or motives.

Narrator

In some plays, a narrator or chorus (group of narrators) stands outside the action and occasionally offers background information, commentary, or other explanations that might be handled by the narrator in a novel or short story. Remember, though, that using a narrator will distance your audience from the action and remind them that they are watching a play.

Stage directions

Stage directions are used to set the scene, suggest what a character is doing while he or she is talking, or indicate sounds or events. Sometimes playwrights include stage directions within a passage of dialogue to give the actor directions.

Script Format

- Begin with a list of the characters in the play. You may want to include a brief description of the more important characters.

- Each time you change to a new location, briefly describe the new setting, at the beginning of the scene.

- Identify who is speaking by writing that character's name in capitals on the left-hand side of the page. (Keep in mind that scripts do not require the use of quotation marks to show that a character is speaking.) Often, playwrights will also use capitals for a character's name mentioned in stage directions.

- Set off stage directions from the dialogue by putting them in parentheses. Use underlining for stage directions if you are handwriting the script; otherwise, use italics.

- Use a long dash (—) or ellipsis points (...) to show that a speech is interrupted or unfinished.

Following is part of a script, as an example.

Books à la Mode

CHARACTERS
Ms. Kemal, *the new librarian*
Ms. Brown, *assistant librarian*
Charlie, *student part-time helper*
Jan, *a boy*
Jameel, *a boy*
Mei-Ling, *a girl*
Myra, *a girl*

TIME: *The present. Friday afternoon.*

SETTING: *A library, in a medium-sized town. Upstage centre is a display of new books. At left is a large reading table. The library counter is at right, with the two librarians' desks behind it.*

AT RISE: Ms. Kemal *and* Charlie *are near the display table, and* Ms. Brown *sits at one desk.*

MS. KEMAL *(Straightening one of the signs and stepping back)*: There, Charlie, I think our display looks wonderful.

CHARLIE: Yes, so do I, Ms. Kemal. It's good to see some new books. I've helped part time in this library since I was in grade eight, but when Ms. Stacy was librarian she never ordered anything but encyclopedias and stuff like that.

MS. KEMAL: They're important too, Charlie, but we have enough of them. When Ms. Stacy retired and Mr. Gregg hired me as the new librarian, I told him I thought we needed some new books. I hope the young people will use the library more — get interested in books — and this is the only way I know. *(She moves a sign a little.)*

CHARLIE: Yes, this display ought to help — and all those posters you had me put in the windows and at school, too.

MS. KEMAL: What about some of your classmates? Do you think I can get them interested in books?

CHARLIE: Well, just since you've been here, you got me interested, and if you got me interested, I figure you can get anyone.

MS. KEMAL *(Laughing)*: It's not as bad as all that, Charlie.

MS. BROWN *(Comes from desk carrying a piece of paper)*: Ms. Kemal, this note of yours saying to make out the file cards in a different way ...

MS. KEMAL: Yes, I know, Ms. Brown, you did it another way, but now I want it done as I've suggested. *(Sound of voices off)*

CHARLIE *(Moving toward stage right)*: Here come some of my friends now.

MS. BROWN *(Shaking her head as she goes back to desk and sits, still shaking her head)*: All right, Ms. Kemal, but I've worked in this library for years and we never did it this way.

MYRA *(Off)*: I could do with a hamburger.

JAMEEL *(Off)*: AND fries!

MEI-LING *(Off)*: Don't look at me.

JAN *(Off)*: Or me either!

Writing a Profile

A profile usually provides insight into the thoughts, feelings, development, or importance of the person you are describing, or the times in which he or she lived.

Select incidents that you feel give insight into your subject's personality. For example, if you want to give the impression that a political leader is untrustworthy, you might describe an incident from the leader's childhood in which he or she was caught cheating on a test. (Someone with a more positive view of the leader might dismiss the incident as unimportant, or omit it altogether.)

Like character sketches, profiles also focus on the character, values, and attitudes of the subject.

Organization of a Profile

Profiles are usually arranged chronologically. As you select the events you think are most relevant, remember the following:

- Try to give a sense of how much time has passed between incidents. For example, if you say "After they moved from the Philippines, the family lived in England for a while and then moved to Canada," your reader has no sense of how much time your subject spent in England. It could be years, months, or days.

- Focus on the facts, but include as much detail as you can to make it interesting. It is the details that will make your reader want to know more. Try to pick up interesting or revealing details by interviewing the subject, or someone close to him or her.

- Decide how you want to present your subject, then choose words and situations that will help to create the impression you want your readers to have of your subject.

- Avoid telling your reader what an incident means or says about the subject. Instead, let the subject's actions and words speak for themselves.

- Use brief quotations (from interviews, books, or magazine articles, for example) to create interest.

- For every quotation, be sure to identify who made the comment, and to use his or her words without changing their meaning. If someone once said that your subject had "an extraordinary ability to get into trouble," don't quote that person as saying your subject had "extraordinary ability."

*Writing is the only thing that,
when I do it, I don't feel I should
be doing something else.*

Gertrude Stein

Doris Anderson: Crusader for Women's Rights

Doris Anderson was born Doris Hilda McCubbin in Calgary, Alberta in 1925, the middle child of five siblings. Her father was a difficult man who did not work much. Her mother had to work hard to support the family. With a difficult home life, Doris applied herself to her studies. She was an excellent student and was persuaded to prepare for a career in "the safe female profession" of teaching. For two years she taught in a rural Alberta school, then returned to the University of Alberta to complete her BA degree in History and English.

McCubbin moved to Toronto and sought work as a journalist. Limited to composing advertising copy, she felt that she was being held back because of her gender. She moved to Europe where she worked for a year in London and Paris selling short stories. In 1951, she was hired as an editorial assistant for *Chatelaine*, a magazine for Canadian women. At the time, *Chatelaine* was a money-losing magazine with a circulation of 460 000. Its pages were filled with helpful household hints — how to make the perfect dessert, how to be a good listener, and how to clean the piano keys with alcohol.

In seven years the hard-working McCubbin finally became the magazine's editor. That same month she married lawyer David Anderson. Her bosses fully expected her to leave the workforce to become a full-time hostess and mother. Doris Anderson did have three children, but she continued to work as editor of *Chatelaine*. She found better writers; produced a more attractive design; and introduced a strong feminist slant in editorials. She commissioned stories on Canada's outdated divorce and abortion laws, on child abuse and poverty, and on discrimination against women in politics and trade unions. Under her leadership, circulation tripled, at a time when other women's magazines continued to falter. More importantly, she was able to challenge traditional wisdom — the Canadian government appointed a Royal Commission on the Status of Women in 1967, after Anderson had begun to demand one in her editorials.

When she was bypassed as editor of the troubled *Maclean's* magazine, and then rejected as publisher of *Chatelaine* in 1977, Doris Anderson abruptly resigned.

In 1978 she was appointed president of the Canadian Advisory Council on the Status of Women, but resigned in 1981 in response to political interference, publicly stating "I don't know why women should be bullied." From 1982 to 1984 she was named president of the National Action Committee on the Status of Women, and continued to fight for equality. After 1984, Doris Anderson continued to promote women's rights as a novelist, broadcaster, and newspaper columnist.

She once wrote: "The women's movement has no armies. It hoards no secret cache of deadly armaments. All we have is numbers." Through her work Anderson helped turn those numbers into a highly effective political force — organized and willing to fight for justice and equality. Doris Anderson, who had made it in a male-dominated business world and still had time to be a caring mother and wife, is a positive role model for the second wave of the Canadian women's movement.

Writing a Speech

If you are asked to give a speech, you might begin by doing the following:

- Decide on the topic (if you have free choice) or decide what aspect(s) of the assigned topic you will cover. You should have a clear goal or purpose.

- Make notes on points and details you might possibly mention.

- Do some research.

- Find some relevant quotations.

> *The art of writing is the art*
> *of applying the seat of the pants*
> *to the seat of the chair.*

Mary Heaton Vorse

Preparing the Speech

When you begin to write your speech, you will find it helpful to do the following:

- Keep in mind your audience — what will interest them? (You may have to give some background to the topic first.)

- Organize your work in an easy-to-follow, logical manner. You should have an introduction and a conclusion.

- Give concrete examples as often as you can.

- Explain any specialized jargon or technical words.

- Work with visual aids such as a transparency, a map, photos, a chart, or the board. (Proofread these before using, for spelling errors.)

- Use appropriate humour. Avoid offensive jokes.

Presenting the Speech

Before you are ready to practise your speech, you should copy it onto small cards. You can do one of two things here: either copy the whole speech or copy a point-form version of the longer speech. The advantage to copying a briefer version of the speech is that you will maintain eye contact with the audience and actually speak your speech, rather than just read it aloud word for word.

It is helpful, too, to remember these points:

- Work your speech until it comes naturally and you can inject gestures and facial expressions.

- Stand with your weight evenly distributed on both feet. If your weight is more on one foot, you will shift frequently during the speech.

- Keep eye contact with the audience.

- Pace your delivery so that listeners can process what you are saying.

- Pause after complicated or important points to give the audience time to think.

- Don't speak in a monotone. Vary your pitch.

- Avoid fillers such as "uh" and "eh."

- Practise delivering your speech into a tape recorder, or in front of a mirror or video camera.

© Lynn Johnston Productions Inc. / Dist. by UNITED FEATURE SYNDICATE, INC.

A Short Speech

Below is an example of how to write a short speech on researching a family tree. Begin by making some notes:

How should a person research his or her family tree?
- interviews with living relatives
- research in church records
- research through public library
- benefits of family-tree research

Then expand your points into sentences.

Following is a final version of this speech.

*I put the words down and
push them a bit.*

Evelyn Waugh

How Should a Person Research His or Her Family Tree?

Suppose one day you were asked for the history of your family. Could you give it? Do you know your family history beyond your grandparents? Do you know where your family came from? Do you know the names and dates of various family members? If you cannot answer "yes" to these questions, you may want to research your family tree. There are three sources you can begin with: living relatives, Mormon Church genealogy centres, and phone-book relatives.

Before you begin to write to distant relatives, you should take time to interview various family members about their knowledge of the family line. You can collect names of people and places where the family came from and write to these people and places just in case they might still be able to give you some family information. If you're unsure if you have any living relatives in a town, you can write to the town secretary and ask that your letter be passed on to people of your surname.

The Mormon Church keeps a research centre in each region, where church members can look up their family background. If you have a Mormon church in your area, call and clear permission for you to look up records that might list your family members.

Particularly helpful are the census reports which are available after 100 years have passed. If you know your family is from somewhere in the British Isles, for example, you can order microfilm versions of the parish registers and of the census reports. These often will list every member of a household and give you confirmation of the family that was living in that area just over 100 years ago.

Once you have exhausted these outlets for information, you might take another step that is highly productive in turning up long-lost relatives. Write a generic letter giving your purpose, your family background as far as you know it, and inviting the recipient to reply. Then, go to the public library in the city nearest you and ask to see phone books from the various cities across Canada. Look up listings with your surname, take down the information, and look up the postal codes when you are finished listing the names. Once you have the complete mailing address for the people listed in various phone books, you are ready to address and mail a letter asking them for more background to the family.

Tracing your family tree is a hobby that can last for years. Travelling to visit places where family has lived can also be a good hobby, especially after a person has retired. Your interest in the family will awaken interest in some family members and bring you closer to your relatives. It is a hobby that could last for years and introduce you to long-lost relatives at the same time.

Making a Presentation

When you are asked to give a presentation, the usual expectations are that you will:

- Do the necessary research.

- Prepare the presentation so that it is organized, clear, and specific — giving facts, reasons, and details as needed.

- Determine what visuals (e.g., overheads, charts, posters, illustrated books with photographs) are needed to support your presentation.

- Explain any technical terms or jargon you are using.

- Allow time for questions.

With a teacher-assigned presentation, the reporting typically should be shared among members of the group. Group members present the report to the class, adding ad-libbed comments as they proceed.

Listed below are questions for developing an oral presentation:

1. What is the presentation task?

2. How might the presentation task be broken down among the various members of the group?

3. What questions or subtopics does each group member have to tackle?

4. What are some points or criteria each group member should consider in framing answers?

5. Have all unfamiliar words been looked up for meaning and pronunciation, using a dictionary?

6. In what order are the questions/answers to be presented?

7. What are some visuals that can be used to make the presentation more interesting?

8. Have enough specific examples been given to back up what is said?

Writing a Research Paper

A research paper involves just what the title suggests: research to support and explain an opinion held by you, the writer. The expectation is that you will present quotations and summaries of research findings that will support your point of view.

Research is usually one of two types: primary and secondary. When using a *primary* source, you are using one of the following:

- any literature you have read initially

- notes you collect

- interviews, surveys, and experiments which you conduct

- performances

- eyewitness reports.

When the source is quoting another source of research, that is called a *secondary* source. Secondary sources may be quoted, usually with a note that indicates the quoted material is in itself a quotation by the writer of a given passage. As well as secondary quotations, secondary sources are reports by other investigators, analyses by other researchers, and critical writing.

Library Catalogue

In libraries, there is always a catalogue (usually accessed by computer) which lists texts available in print or electronic form. Each book is listed under at least three headings: author, title, and subject. In computer files, you may also be able to search by contents, by key words, or in other ways. Your choices will be listed on the main menu.

Encyclopedia

Libraries typically have basic encyclopedias such as *The Canadian Encyclopedia*, *Encyclopaedia Britannica*, *World Book*, *Collier's*, and *Current Biography*. These yield basic information about a subject or person, and are a good place to start any print search. Listings are often brief and introductory in nature. The listing may also suggest other related topics and other resources.

As well, there are specialized encyclopedias such as *Reader's Encyclopedia* and *Halliwell's Filmgoers' Encyclopedia* which give more specialized information about a person or the subject.

Magazine

Reader's Guide to Periodical Literature and the *Canadian Periodical Index* are good basic resources for accessing recent print articles in magazines such as *Reader's Digest, Time,* and *Maclean's.*

Internet

Through sites on the World Wide Web, you can discover more information about your research topic. These sources are usually more up-to-date than books or periodicals. There is a disadvantage, however. Since anyone, including businesses with vested interests, can post information on a Web site, what you read is not always accurate — you must check all facts against at least one other source.

Below are some popular search engines. If you can't find what you want with one of them, or if a site no longer exists, try a different one.

- AltaVista www.altavista.com/
- Canada.com www.canada.com/
- Excite www.excite.com/
- HotBot www.hotbot.lycos.com/
- LookSmart www.looksmart.com/
- Lycos www.lycos.com/
- Web Crawler www.webcrawler.com/
- Yahoo! www.yahoo.com/
- Yahoo! Canada ca.yahoo.com/

The University at Albany Libraries and *refdesk* are sites that offer excellent research strategies.

- www.albany.edu/library/internet/research.html
- www.refdesk.com/toc.html

As with library catalogues, start by entering a key word or phrase. (When you enter a phrase, put quotation marks around it. Otherwise, the resulting list will include all the Web pages that contain ANY of the words in the phrase.)

If you find the list of Web sites is long, try eliminating those posted by individuals.

.com	*business or company site*
.edu	*educational site*
.gc.ca	*Canadian government site*
.gov	*government (usually U.S.) site*
.in	*international organization site*
.org	*not-for-profit organization site*
.ca	*network service site*

CD-ROM

Portable databases such as *National Geographic* can be read on computer and can provide a reliable, comprehensive source for research. Some encyclopedias and reference books are also available on CD-ROMs.

Interview

Interviews are a good way to get expert opinions. The first-hand information given in an interview makes a topic come alive. Here are some tips to consider when handling interviews:

- Decide how you will conduct the interview: by phone, by mail/e-mail, or in person. Never meet a person alone; choose a public place, and bring a partner.

- Do some background research in the topic. You will be able to ask more specific questions if you know your topic well.

- Formulate questions that only your subject can answer. Try to word your questions so that they cannot be answered with a simple *yes* or *no.*

- Take notes, or use a tape recorder (with permission), for direct quotations. Immediately after the interview, read over your notes, clarify any scribbles or abbreviations, and jot down remembered ideas.

Very soon after the interview, write a letter thanking the person.

Evaluating the Usefulness of Sources

You want information from sources, especially from the Net, to be as useful and relevant as possible. To this end, then, you might consider the following:

- Is the information relevant to your topic?

- Is the author an authority in the field? What are his or her credentials?

- Might the author have a vested interest that slants the presentation?

- How recent is the source?

- Is the source long enough to provide necessary detail to support its main points?

- Does the source give you other articles or books to look up? Is the source cross-referenced elsewhere?

- For which audience is the source intended?

- If the source is electronic, who has posted the document or page? Is the person or group who posted this page credible? For example, a Web site with a .edu (that is, educational) address is more likely to be objective than a .com (that is, commercial) site.

Quotations and Citations

While doing research, it is helpful to copy direct quotations onto small cards and to note the details of the source at the bottom of each card. With the quotations on different cards, you can easily shuffle the order around, and eliminate those you do not wish to use.

Longer quotations

Longer quotations are separated from the essay body, double-spaced, and indented from the left and right on each line. No quotation marks are needed because the placement of the quoted material already indicates that it has been quoted. You can edit a longer quotation by substituting ellipsis points (three spaced periods) within square brackets for words cut out. For example,

> You can edit [. . .] by substituting ellipsis points [. . .] for words
>
> cut out.

To show that you have omitted a line or lines in the middle of a poetry quotation, use a line of spaced periods about the same length as the line of the quoted poem.

> Sunset and evening star,
>
> And one clear call for me!
>
> [. . . . .]
>
> When that which drew from out the boundless deep
>
> Turns again home.

Shorter quotations

When you use a shorter quotation, it is best to embed it in a sentence, using opening and closing double quotation marks.

*Everyone is talented, original,
and has something to say.*

Brenda Ueland

Citations

There are many styles for documenting sources — MLA, APA, University of Chicago, and others. You can find reference books for all styles in libraries and bookstores. The examples in this handbook are given in MLA. In this style, you cite your source by giving the author's name and page reference in parentheses, within the text.

Below is an example — from a research paper on *Hamlet* — of one longer quotation and one shorter quotation.

In Act 3, scene iii, Hamlet is on his way to see his mother in her closet. He comes across Claudius, who is attempting to pray. Hamlet considers killing Claudius at that point, but he does not because Claudius is at prayer and might go to heaven. What Hamlet does not know, and what we later find out, is that Claudius is unable to pray and is just as burdened with sin as at any other time. Critic K.D. Wilson observes that:

> Hamlet errs when he declines to kill Claudius, who appears to be at prayer. In fact, Claudius is unwilling to give up his ill-gotten gains and therefore cannot genuinely repent.
>
> (Wilson 81)

Wilson points out that Claudius' main problem is this: he cannot genuinely repent as long as he is enjoying the benefits of his sin. Therefore, if Hamlet had killed him, Claudius would have gone to hell with all his sins fresh on his soul. Another critic explains that "Hamlet makes an error [. . .] that brings about the tragic deaths at the end of the play." (Rosewood 234)

Footnotes

Instead of these in-text citations, other styles use footnotes — a small raised number at the end of source material, and a footnote with a matching number at the bottom of the page, or on a separate page (called *Endnotes*) immediately before the *Bibliography* page.

If this corresponding footnote is the first documentation of a work, it describes that work completely, giving the name of the author, the title of the book, details of the publication, and the page number of the quotation. (See the following page for samples from various sources.)

Avoiding Plagiarism

You may choose to paraphrase a quotation, especially if it is very long. If you are paraphrasing, you are putting the section into your own words. Some people mistakenly believe that if they change the wording of a quotation, it is no longer quoted material and does not need to be acknowledged. That is incorrect. As long as the ideas belong to someone else, acknowledgment is still needed, even though you change the wording. Plagiarism (using others' work and claiming it as your own) is a very serious academic offence.

Documenting Sources

At the end of your research essay, make a list of the sources actually cited in your text, on a separate page titled *Works Cited*. Instead of *Works Cited*, other styles sometimes use the term *Bibliography*.

Either way, this is a list of the sources used, arranged alphabetically by author's surname. For each citation, indent all lines except the first line. (See p. 91 for an example.)

On the following page are sample citations for various sources.

A Book

Roussakis, Roula T. *Researching Your Family Tree.* Toronto: Donvale Press, 1998.

A Work with Two or Three Authors

Eshpeter, James, and Harold Kotter. *Ways to Improve the Environment without Great Cost.* Toronto: Gage, 1998.

An Anthology/Compilation

Downar, Mei-Li, ed. *Scanning Techniques.* Toronto: Gage, 2000.

An Article or a Chapter within a Source

Sexton, Deborah June. "Finding the Branches on Your Family Tree." *Family Tree Research.* Toronto: Webline Press,1994.

A Newspaper Article

Thompson, David. "Rock Forever." *Edmonton Bulletin* 17 Mar., 1998.

A Film

Citizen Kane. Dir. Orson Welles. RKO, 1941.

A Television Program

Gardening Made Easy. CTV. Regina. 17 Jan., 2000.

A Web Site

Delaney, Don. *Projects for the Gifted Student.* October 1998 <www.gifted.students.@ecs.edmonton.ab.ca>.

A CD-ROM

Kelly, Mortimer. "Discovering Hamlet." *Shakespeare's Plays.* CD-ROM. Vers. 2.0. New York: Oppenheimer, 1998.

E-mail

Smith, Marilyn. "Re: Research Project." E-mail to Fred James. 17 October, 1999.

An Interview

Jones, Dr. Epatha. Personal interview. 16 April, 1995.

The following example of a research paper is an analysis of a poem. Here is the poem, for reference.

Crossing the Bar

Sunset and evening star,
> And one clear call for me!
And may there be no moaning of the bar,
> When I put out to sea,

But such a tide as moving seems asleep,
> Too full for sound and foam,
When that which drew from out the boundless deep
> Turns again home.

Twilight and evening bell,
> And after that the dark!
And may there be no sadness of farewell,
> When I embark;

For tho' from out our bourne of Time and Place
> The flood may bear me far,
I hope to see my Pilot face to face
> When I have crost the bar.

Alfred, Lord Tennyson

Face to Face with "Crossing the Bar"

Scott Davies

English 1A3

Ms. N. Vlesto

23 March, 1999

Alfred, Lord Tennyson's "Crossing the Bar" is one of the poet's later works. This significant, reflective, and well-constructed poem has been on the receiving end of much praise, and is generally held in high regard. "Crossing the Bar" views the transience of life with an inner tranquillity. The completeness of the poem's structure provides the means for an effective presentation of Tennyson's thoughts. One critic has noted that "Crossing the Bar" is "Tennyson's most famous description of the soul's return to its beginnings" (Pitt 242). To capture the meaning of this statement, it is important, first, to get an understanding of the background of the poem.

"Crossing the Bar" first appeared in *Demeter and Other Poems* (1889). It had been written two months earlier in October 1889 when Tennyson was crossing the Solent, travelling from Aldworth to Farringford. Prior to this, at the age of 81, Tennyson had been seriously ill for an extended period of time. In April or May of 1889, after his recovery from his illness, his nurse suggested he write a hymn (Ricks 253). Apparently, he had the "Moaning of the Bar" in his mind before reaching Farringford, and he "began and finished [writing] it in twenty minutes" (Lang and Shannon 414). After hearing the poem the evening after it was written, his son proclaimed "Crossing the Bar" to be the crown of his father's life's work. Lord Tennyson replied, "It came in a moment" (Tennyson 391).

On publication, it was immediately recognized as one of Tennyson's most successful lyrics. A great number of critics and fans have agreed on this, and Tennyson's son has been quoted as saying, "That is one of the most beautiful poems ever written" (Ricks 251). One critic argues that the poem is a reconciliation of many of Tennyson's earlier poems (Ricks 253). A few days prior to his death, Tennyson instructed his son to put "Crossing the Bar" at the end of all collections of his work (Hill 496).

The meaning of "Crossing the Bar" is of great interest, because the poem, in a deeper sense, exemplifies Tennyson's last testament to the world (Buckley 253). First, the image of a bar — a sandbank across a harbour mouth — is a metaphor for the framework drawn by our perceptions (Hair 79). To cross the bar, one must transcend this boundary. The first stanza begins with a declaration of a "clear call" amid the casual "sunset and evening star" for the speaker to go beyond the boundary implied by the title. The "bar" is immediately established as the end of life; therefore, death is implied. This is followed by a wish not to hear the forlorn sound of the ocean pounding on a sand bar at a harbour-mouth when he puts out to sea. Here, the speaker is wishing for there to be no mournfulness at the occasion of his death. The metaphor of the poem develops as the second stanza speaks more about the sea, which represents the eternity from which the soul emerges and to which it returns naturally.

The third stanza mirrors the first stanza. The speaker describes a certain awareness of approaching death in the twilight, amid the sound of evening bells. After the sound of the bells, there is only darkness to be found at the end of life. The use of exclamation marks here and in the first stanza signify the speaker's enthusiasm for the experience. He again emphatically wishes for there to be no pity as his life ends. In the final stanza, the speaker establishes a belief in the afterlife, as he asserts the flood will carry him beyond the "bourne of Time and Place." Most significantly, he expresses the wish to meet his "Pilot" in the afterlife. The "Pilot" has been defined by the poet as "That Divine and Unseen who is always guiding us" (Buckley 243). The presence of the Pilot is vital to the understanding of the poem. Tennyson explained: "The Pilot has been on board all the while, but in the dark I have not seen him" (Hill 496). The speaker has embarked at evening, but upon the crossing of the bar, he hopes to see his Pilot "face to face" as the dawn's light breaks, and no longer through the hazy darkness. He hopes that the mystery surrounding his creation and the meaning of his life will be clarified at this point. Being reunited with nature and his Creator provides an optimistic undercurrent to the speaker's passing. Clearly, Tennyson's metaphors of the sea and darkness effectively convey his optimistic perception of life.

Tennyson's effectiveness in presenting his thoughts owes much to the structure of "Crossing the Bar." The integrity of the work as an entire unit is remarkable. By balancing the first two stanzas against the third and the fourth, Tennyson has created a poem with its own self-sustained completeness. The rhymes are interwoven — the end line stanza rhyme is ABAB. The long third line followed by the short concluding line of each quatrain reinforces the rhyme. The meter is iambic, with the number of stresses in each line varying from two to five, giving the freedom that is desirable when working within the ABAB stanza form. The repetitions and subtle variations in metre establish the poem's relaxed movement, integral in creating the acceptant mood of the poem (Buckley 243).

Impressively, the imagery and figures of speech throughout the work are altogether consistent and functional. The choice of the personification "Pilot" is notably intriguing. It may be considered odd that the speaker has apparently not seen his pilot, as do most voyagers, by the time they reach the bar. Because Tennyson uses the term "Pilot" to describe his Creator, he is implying (via the metaphor) that he has seen his Creator, but not in the full light that the expression "face to face" suggests. Acknowledging Tennyson's command of poetic techniques in "Crossing the Bar," the Duke of Argyll wrote that it was "perfect in [. . .] several ways and such as no other man could have written" (Lang and Shannon 438).

Under close analysis, "Crossing the Bar" can easily be celebrated as a vital, philosophical, and well-refined poem. The importance of the poem to Tennyson, his critics, and his fans is obvious. The work presents his thoughts on death in an engaging manner. Assessment of the poem's structure reveals the perfection that the Duke of Argyll (and many others) have observed in its sixteen lines. "Poetry," Lord Tennyson wrote, "should be the flower and fruit of a man's life, in whatever stage of it, to be a worthy offering to the world" (Tennyson 392).

Works Cited

Abrams, M.H. *The Norton Anthology of English Literature, 6th ed.* New York: W.W. Norton & Co., Inc., 1996.

Buckley, Jerome Hamilton. *Tennyson: The Growth of a Poet.* Cambridge: Harvard University Press, 1969.

Hair, Donald S. *Tennyson's Language.* Toronto: University of Toronto Press, 1991.

Hill, Robert W., Jr., ed. *Tennyson's Poetry.* New York: W.W. Norton & Company, Inc., 1971.

Lang, Cecil Y., and Edgar F. Shannon Jr., eds. *The Letters of Alfred, Lord Tennyson.* Vol. 3. Oxford: Clarendon Press, 1990.

Pitt, Valerie. *Tennyson Laureate.* Toronto: University of Toronto Press, 1962.

Ricks, Christopher, ed. *The Poems of Tennyson.* Vol. 3. Berkeley: University of California Press, 1969.

Tennyson, Hallam Lord, ed. *The Works of Tennyson.* Vol. 7. Westport: Greenwood Press, Publishers, 1908.

Writing a Position Paper

A position paper is commonly written for Social Studies/History courses. Typically, a position paper explores the complexity and significance of an issue.

Usually, you cover the complexity first, by presenting at least three standpoints on the issue. Two of the standpoints should describe the extreme views. The third should provide a middle ground position. Each of these three standpoints should be represented by strong arguments in its favour.

In the conclusion of a position paper — dealing with the significance of the issue — you should explain why the issue is important or relevant, what its ramifications are, and why it is important to have an opinion on the issue. Normally, you present your own position at this point (which may agree with one of the previous three views), and back it up with evidence.

© Sidney Harris.

Letting Slip the Dogs of War

Should nations ever go to war? There is probably no issue that is more important than this one. In his book Out of Control: Global Turmoil on the Eve of the Twenty-first Century (1993), Zbigniew Brzezinski estimated that the wars of the twentieth century had killed about 87 500 000 people — 33 500 000 soldiers and 54 000 000 civilians. Since 1993, wars in Rwanda, Chechnya, Kosovo, East Timor, Liberia, and other trouble spots have added to Brzezinski's staggering total. These figures suggest that, in the twentieth century, no issue has affected humanity more tragically than war. Governments are regularly forced into situations in which they must decide whether or not to take up arms against another country. Millions of lives and the survival of a nation may depend on such a decision.

The issue of whether or not to go to war is also a complex one. This complexity stems from the variety of positions on the question and the compelling nature of arguments on all sides of the debate. On the one extreme, pacifists maintain that war must be avoided at all costs. It is hard to dismiss their claim that war causes more misery and destruction than any other human activity. At the other extreme, militarists favour a warlike approach in foreign policy. They argue that human nature is warlike and that pacifist nations are in danger of losing their independence to aggressive countries. The middle position belongs to those who believe in some version of what is called the "just war" doctrine. Those who embrace it believe that nations are justified in going to war in some circumstances, but not in others.

After careful thought, the traditional "just war" doctrine that was pioneered by Augustine of Hippo and Thomas Aquinas seems to offer the soundest guidance on the issue of military conflict. It is certainly more rational than the extreme ideologies of militarism or pacifism. Should nations ever go to war? The pacifist response to the question is too naive. The militarist response inevitably leads to disaster. The approach recommended by the traditional "just war" doctrine is both realistic and ethical. It states that a nation is justified in going to war whenever it has a just cause and the right intention and a reasonable chance of success.

Although many pacifist beliefs are admirable, it would be foolish to embrace the ideology of pacifism. In fact, no real-world state ever has. Even India could not bring itself to follow the teachings of its great pacifist leader Mohandas (Mahatma) Gandhi. Nations will not commit themselves to pacifism because states that have appeared to do so have not done well in the global arena. Pacifism makes no sense unless all nations have embraced pacifism. As long as aggressor-states such as Saddam Hussein's Iraq or Slobodan Milosevic's Serbia exist, nations should prepare for war if they want peace. The wisdom of being prepared was demonstrated by the situation in Europe before World War II. In 1938, Great Britain was populated mostly by pacifists who had learned to hate war during the Great War of 1914-18. In fact, Britain's prime minister Neville Chamberlain, and most of the members of his government, became peacemongers in the effort to maintain the support of Britain's pacifist majority. In the end, they adopted one of the pacifist's main tools — the policy of appeasement. Chamberlain's government chose to give in to an aggressive Nazi Germany at the Munich Conference in 1938 rather than risk war. Chamberlain's pacifist approach was very popular at the time, but became much criticized later — when its consequences became evident. The major problem with appeasement was that it allowed history's worst warmonger — Adolf Hitler — the time and space he needed to build up a huge army and plunge the world into the horrors of World War II and the

Holocaust. If Chamberlain had been willing to confront Hitler with strength in 1938, instead of trying to appease him with a slice of Czechoslovakia, Britain and the world might not have had to experience the Second World War. This is not to suggest that Chamberlain necessarily should have gone to war against Germany in 1938 to stop German aggression and imperialism, but he should have been more willing, at least, to use confrontational foreign policy approaches such as brinkmanship or economic sanctions — strategies which pacifists are generally reluctant to risk. As Edmund Burke noted, "The only thing necessary for the triumph of evil is [. . .] to do nothing." Doing nothing or almost nothing in the face of military aggression is exactly what many pacifists support. Ultimately, if Britain had not been so naively pacifist during the 1930s, it probably would have been able to deal more effectively with Hitler and to prevent World War II.

The militaristic position on the issue of whether or not to go to war is just as short-sighted as the pacifist one. Warmongers are too willing to look for military solutions to their political and economic problems. Hitler and Mussolini could have tried to improve national prosperity by increasing trade with other countries. Instead, they chose to try to conquer and exploit other countries to gain what they wanted. Usually, military aggressiveness involves a country in war and leads to catastrophe. Hitler's militarism resulted in the deaths of millions of Germans and the destruction of every German city. Benito Mussolini's militarism led to the same results for Italy. Countries that seek military glory on the battlefield sow the seeds of their own destruction. Other nations will ultimately band together against the aggressor. This fact has been demonstrated again and again throughout history. For example, this lesson was learned the hard way by Napoleonic France in the nineteenth century.

A nation must be prepared to go to war if it desires freedom, peace, and security. Some wars are necessary, just as some occasions require self-defense. A nation, however, should take up arms only when it can affirmatively respond to all of the following questions:

1) Is war a last resort?

2) Is the cause just?

3) Are the nation's intentions honourable?

4) Will the war be waged in a lawful way?

5) Is victory probable?

6) Will war result in less death and destruction than surrender to an aggressor?

First of all, war is dangerous and destructive. As American General William Tecumseh Sherman noted, "It is hell." Nations should use diplomacy, economic sanctions, and brinkmanship before they ever resort to war. Secondly, nations are only justified in going to war when they have a just cause. The only two just causes that are currently recognized by the UN Charter are self-defense and collective security against aggression. Stopping gross violations of human rights, such as genocide or ethnic cleansing, is one other example of a just cause. Thirdly, a nation should not go to war for any other motives, such as revenge or economic gain. Fourthly, only military actions that conform to the rules of war can be just. A nation should not commit war crimes in order to fight or win a war. For instance, an army is never justified in targeting civilians or mistreating prisoners of war. Fifthly, there is no sense in making war if one cannot win the war. Bloodless submission is almost always preferable to surrender caused by massive bloodletting. After all, what good resulted from Belgium's stand against the German juggernaut in World War I? Finally, when a country goes to war, it should always be the lesser of two evils. For instance, if war means global nuclear warfare then war should never be declared. A nation is only justified in going to war when it is prepared to follow these six guidelines of the traditional "just war" doctrine.

If one requires a good example of a just war, look no further than the Allies' war against the Axis powers in World War II. An Axis victory in this war would have led to unimaginable horrors for the human race. Canada was only one among many nations which were right to oppose fascist tyranny in Europe and Asia. Canadian motives for going to war were honourable. What did a nation like Canada have to gain from the war? What ulterior motives did Canadians have for fighting the three warmongering Axis powers? This was a defensive war to stop aggression and to liberate millions of people who were suffering under tyrannical regimes.

We live in a world where most people recognize that murder is wrong — but also that killing in self-defense is sometimes necessary. This principle of personal morality must also be applied to international relations. Just as some killings are justified, some wars are justified — provided that they are defensive in nature. Pacifists seem to suggest that killing in self-defense is just as wrong as cold-blooded murder. Even a small child can see that this is nonsense. On the other extreme, militarists fail to see war as evil under any circumstances. These warmongers reject the idea that states, like human beings, should follow ethical principles. This attitude can make the world a cruel, violent, and dangerous place for human beings. Violence should always be a last resort; but it is sometimes unavoidable. In fact, given that armed conflict seems to be a constant in human affairs, it seems to be inevitable. But nations can wage war with a clean conscience when they conduct it in a moral way. The traditional "just war" doctrine provides them with guidelines for doing so. The global community should follow these guidelines if it wants to be more secure. They offer a practical way to work toward the peaceful world of pacifists' dreams.

Writing a Science Experiment Report

The basic pattern of a lab report is as follows.

Purpose

State what the experiment is attempting to show.

Problem

Give a concise statement of what the experiment is trying to do, often in question form. Background, context, and variables can be stated here.

Hypothesis

State the outcome or results expected regarding the hypothesis tested.

Experimental Design

List the steps of the experiment, mentioning variables.

Materials

List the equipment required to perform the experiment.

Procedure

Give a step-by-step explanation of the experiment: what the experimenter does, the records, safety precautions taken, and methods for waste disposal.

Observations

Present your observations, preferably in the form of a table. Include expected and unexpected results.

Analysis

Give a concise statement of what you have shown or demonstrated, including calculations.

Conclusion

This is your interpretation of what has happened with respect to the problem statement.

Evaluation

In this section, comment (where relevant) on the accuracy of the experimental design, the appropriateness of the hypothesis, the validity of the results, the handling of the experiment, and the percent error or difference.

Investigating Photosynthesis

Purpose
The photosynthesis equation states that carbon dioxide and water will combine to make glucose and oxygen in a plant if light is present. We will show that this equation for photosynthesis is adequate.

Problem
Can we show glucose is present in the leaves of a plant?

Hypothesis
Photosynthesis occurs in the leaves so, according to the photosynthesis equation, there should be glucose in the leaves of a plant.

Experimental Design
We will extract the juices from a plant leaf by mashing the leaf with a few drops of water. Any glucose in the leaf should be released. The Benedict's test indicates the presence of glucose, so we will conduct this test on the mashed leaves.

Manipulated Variable – plant type
Responding Variable – presence of glucose

Materials
5 green leaves (various plants)
6 test tubes
mortar and pestle
250 mL beaker
hot plate
Benedict's solution
5% glucose solution

<u>Procedure</u>
1. Mash plant leaf with a few drops of water.
2. Place mashed leaf in a test tube; add 5 drops Benedict's solution.
3. Add water until the test tube is approximately 3/4 full.
4. Observe and record the colour of the leaf.
5. Place test tube in a beaker of boiling water on the hot plate.
6. Repeat for all five leaves.
7. Fill the sixth test tube about 3/4 full with glucose solution. Add 5 drops Benedict's solution to this test tube. Observe and record the colour of the solution. Place test tube in a beaker of boiling water on the hot plate.
8. Observe and record any colour changes in all six test tubes.

<u>Observations</u>

	Original Colour	Colour After Heating
Pine Needle	Light Blue	Light Blue
Oak Leaf	Light Blue	Light Blue
Tomato Leaf	Light Blue	Green
Rose Leaf	Light Blue	Green
Begonia Leaf	Light Blue	Green
Water and Glucose	Light Blue	Orange

<u>Analysis</u>
The water and glucose test showed that, in the presence of glucose, Benedict's solution turns from blue to orange.

In two of the leaves (pine needle and oak leaf) there was no change in the colour of the Benedict's solution, indicating glucose is not present in these leaves.

In the test on tomato, rose, and begonia leaves a colour change occurred. The Benedict's solution changed from blue to green. These changes indicate that glucose is present in the leaves. The change to green indicates the concentration of glucose is less than 5% as in the control experiment (test tube 6).

Conclusion
These results are not conclusive. In some leaves we have some evidence that glucose exists, in others the test shows no glucose. Therefore, we cannot say glucose is in the leaves of plants.

Evaluation
This experiment is judged to be adequate, but insufficient. The procedures are simple and easy to follow. The results are easy to see, but the evidence provided is not sufficient to solve the problem.

A possible source of error may have been introduced by not cleaning the mortar after crushing each leaf. This may have caused glucose from one leaf to enter the test tube for the next one.

Business Writing

Résumé

Most full-time jobs require a résumé from job applicants. The function of a résumé is to show the prospective employer that you are capable of putting information together to make it easier for the prospective employer to judge whether or not you would be a good employee.

A résumé does more for you than most application forms will. An application form provides an introduction of your most essential information. A résumé provides a comprehensive and systematic overview of your experience and your qualifications.

Below is a sample organization for a résumé. The categories shown here can be modified to suit the individual's background and experience.

Personal Data
Name

Address

Postal code

Phone number

Fax number

E-mail address

Education
- List the grade level you have completed and indicate the pattern of study you are following (general/academic; university/technical institute/community college).

- Indicate any specific school-related skills or certificates you have acquired that would make you more employable.

Employment History
- Date of employment

- Position, Employer/Company

- Duties (listed in point form)

Repeat this pattern as often as you have jobs to report.

If you have had few jobs, then report on areas of significant responsibility — babysitting, cutting grass, or doing odd jobs. The idea is to show that you have had responsibilities.

Related Experience

- List any skills you have gained at home or through your part-time work — using a keyboard, using a calculator, answering telephones, etc.

- List hobbies, organizations belonged to, and volunteer experience, as well as other languages spoken. Some résumés (like the one on the following page) will give separate lists of skills, organizations, volunteer experience, and interests.

References

Usually, you give two or three names — neighbours, previous employers, and teachers. Be sure to ask first if you can use their name as a reference. Do not list friends or relatives.

List the name, position, and business of each reference and their phone numbers as below.

- Name of reference person
- Position, Company
- Address with postal code
- Phone number

Alternatively, indicate that references are available on request. (See page 105.)

Format

Leave spaces between headings and underline or boldface those headings. Each section should be clear and the information eye-catching.

Following is an example of a reasonably informative résumé.

Pearl Gonzalez
840 - 978 Street
Clearview, Alberta
T7Z 3W7
(123) 456-7890

Education

J. K. Strong Composite High School: graduation with honours, June 1999

University of Alberta: completed first year in BA program; expected graduation April 2003

Work History

July to August 1999
General employee, Wilson's Housewares
Was part of the set-up crew for the construction of a new store. Tasks included setting up store fixtures, unloading trucks, stocking shelves and other storage spaces, preparing the garden centre, and setting up store displays.

December 1999 to present
Weekend Supervisor, Rollerbladin'
Involved in the maintenance and operation of an indoor rollerblading facility. Tasks include overseeing co-workers' duties, DJing, distributing and repairing rental rollerblades, and operating an admission and concession area.

Skills

– editing and research

– excellent English skills (have been asked to enter Honours English program)

– public relations

– explaining and interpreting

– planning, arranging, assembling

– Macintosh and IBM computer operation, programming, and on-line experience

– music: bass clarinet, guitar, piano

– computer-aided design — posters/publicity

Organizations

- Dan Smith Concert Band: grade 9

- J. K. Strong Concert, Dixieland, and Jazz Bands: grades 11 and 12

- Clearview Wind Ensemble: March 1998 to August 1998

Volunteer Experience

Summer 1994 and 1995
Wilson's Golf Tournament
Involved in ball-spotting and golf cart preparation.

December 1997
Clearview Christmas Bureau
Involved in envelope-stuffing for the annual campaign.

Interests

I take pleasure in writing and playing music, and keeping active with my friends. I enjoy working out, bowling, and rollerblading. In my spare time at home, I enjoy using the home computer for both work and entertainment. I am also casually involved as a guitarist in a band.

References

Available upon request.

Standard Business Letter

In the business world, there are several acceptable formats for business letters. If you are hired by a company, you should ask for a model of the format they use. Below is the most common format, called Block style.

16 Bolsover Lane
Barr Harbour, NS B2Z 1R6

October 25, 20—

Mr. David G. Carli
Executive Vice President
Letter Writers of Canada, Ltd.
9505 Brown Avenue
Truehaven, ON M2W 8K9

Dear Mr. Carli:

Re: Business Letter

The complete address of the writer (called the *heading*) is placed flush with the left margin of the letter, keyed one line under the other with no indenting. (In the business world, this return address would be the company letterhead, and might be centred on the page.) Below this is one line with the current date. The name and address of the person to whom the letter is written (called the *inside address*) goes next. There is no end punctuation on the addresses.

The letter opens with a *greeting*, usually *Dear _____*. The first paragraph after the greeting states what the letter is about, or the purpose of the letter.

Next comes the *body* of the letter. Note that there is a space left between paragraphs, and there is no indenting in the letter body.

There is usually a short closing paragraph, often thanking the reader for reading and responding to the letter.

The *complimentary closing* begins with *Sincerely* (or *Yours sincerely* or *Sincerely yours*). The writer's name, followed by any title or reference initials, is keyed below, leaving a double space for the signature.

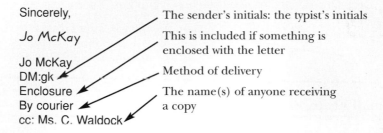

Sincerely,   The sender's initials: the typist's initials

Jo McKay   This is included if something is
enclosed with the letter

Jo McKay
DM:gk   Method of delivery
Enclosure   The name(s) of anyone receiving
By courier   a copy
cc: Ms. C. Waldock

E-mail

One of the newest forms of communication, e-mail (short form for electronic mail), can be formal or very informal. The term refers to any of the various programs that send and receive messages over a network. Specifically, the term also means the electronic correspondence between two or more parties. Below is a sample e-mail:

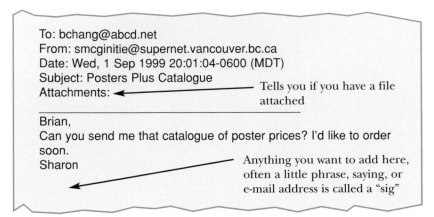

To: bchang@abcd.net
From: smcginitie@supernet.vancouver.bc.ca
Date: Wed, 1 Sep 1999 20:01:04-0600 (MDT)
Subject: Posters Plus Catalogue
Attachments: ◄————————— Tells you if you have a file
                                          attached

Brian,
Can you send me that catalogue of poster prices? I'd like to order soon.
Sharon ————————► Anything you want to add here,
                          often a little phrase, saying, or
                          e-mail address is called a "sig"

E-mail Features

- Workplace e-mails are electronic internal memos and should be written in that style.

- First names and a friendly positive tone are acceptable in e-mails; e.g., Hi Fred; Cheers, Cam.

- Missing words, misspelled words, and bad grammar are not acceptable.

- Many users don't like attachment files, mass e-mailings, and unsolicited e-mail.

- E-mail should not be too personal or angry in tone. For example, the use of capital letters for entire words is interpreted as shouting.

- If your e-mail is urgent, say so in the Subject heading.

E-mail Acronyms

BFN: bye for now

BTW: by the way

FAQ: frequently asked questions

FYI: for your information

HTH: hope this helps

IMHO: in my humble opinion

IOW: in other words

NRN: no reply necessary

TIA: thanks in advance

TTYL: talk to you later

TYVM: thank you very much

WYSIWYG: what you see is what you get

A letter of invitation can either be brief and straightforward, or slightly longer, depending on the occasion and the recipient. Suppose, for example, that you were working for your school's student council and you were assigned the task of writing a letter to parents, inviting them to come to the Awards Night. Your letter might look like this:

> 12233-44 Street
> Norton, Manitoba
> R7L 2G9
> May 30, 2000
>
> Mr. and Mrs. P. Malhotra
> 332211-44 Avenue
> Norton, Manitoba
> R6H 3C7
>
> Dear Mr. and Mrs. Malhotra,
>
> On June 16, Nalwen High School will host an Awards Night. You are cordially invited to attend the ceremony, which will honour the school's most outstanding achievers.
>
> The evening will honour 102 students who have made an outstanding achievement in the areas of scholastics, participation, leadership, or athletics. The evening will also feature a brief concert by "The Mellow Tones," our school band.
>
> The evening will begin at 7 p.m. and likely will end about 10:30. We would appreciate a call to Elana Dubois, our school secretary, at 555-3333, to say if you are planning to attend. Your support would be much appreciated.
>
> Sincerely,
>
> *Stephen Student*
>
> Stephen Student
> Member-at-large, Student Council
> Nalwen High School

Thank-you Letter

A thank-you letter can be brief and straightforward. The aim is to express appreciation for the contributions of a special guest.

12233-44 Street
Norton, Manitoba
R7L 2G
June 19, 2000

Mr. Azim Fortin
21764-44 Avenue
Norton, Manitoba
R6H 3C5

Dear Mr. Azim Fortin,

This letter is to express our thanks for your contribution to our Awards Night. Your speech was appropriately inspiring and memorable. Thank you for helping to make this a special evening.

Sincerely,

Stephen Student

Stephen Student
Member-at-large, Student Council
Nalwen High School

Part 3

Conventions of Writing

Paragraph

A paragraph is a group of sentences that develops one aspect of a topic. Paragraphs are the essential building blocks of essays; they must have five features in order to be successful:

- **a topic sentence**
  The topic sentence expresses the main idea being developed.

- **unity**
  All sentences should relate to the topic sentence.

- **development**
  Paragraphs have to be long enough to deal meaningfully with the topic sentence.

- **points/ideas and examples**
  These create the development of the topic and provide evidence or support.

- **smooth transitions**
  Transitions are needed from sentence to sentence, and from the previous paragraph to the following paragraph. Here is a list of linking words that are helpful in making transitions.

For...	Try these linking words...
cause-effect	as a result, because, consequently, for this reason, however, since, therefore, thus
comparison/ contrast	although, by contrast, compared with (to), even though, however, in the same way, likewise, on the other hand, similarly
conclusion	finally, in conclusion, in short, in summary, then, therefore, to conclude, to summarize, to sum up
emphasis	again, also, equally important, furthermore, in addition, in fact, moreover
explanation	because, for example, for instance, for this reason, furthermore, in addition, in other words, in particular, since, specifically
importance	equally important, finally, first (second, third), lastly, most importantly, next
time	after, afterward, as, at last, before, during, finally, just then, later, meanwhile, next, once, since, soon, suddenly, then, while

Below is a sample paragraph, on a key speech by Macbeth. Notice all the above features at work:

In Act I, scene vii, Macbeth reconsiders whether he should murder Duncan. At first, he wishes that the assassination of the king would not have consequences and that the murder would be the "be-all and end-all." However, Macbeth is a thoughtful man who knows that rebellion will lead to more rebellion, and that he himself might end up being killed by someone else. Besides, the thane says that there are three reasons to be loyal to Duncan. First, he is related to the king and should be his loyal subject. Second, he is also Duncan's host and hosts don't normally kill guests! Third, he says Duncan is a meek man whose wrongful death will cause much unnecessary grief and suffering. He concludes that he has nothing but his own ambition as motivation for murder and that is probably not reason enough to rebel.

FOXTROT © Bill Amend. Reprinted with permission of UNIVERSAL PRESS SYNDICATE. All rights reserved.

Sentence

A sentence is a group of words that expresses a complete thought. Six elements of successful sentences are.

- **clearness**
  No part of the sentence should be awkward or ambiguous. If you suspect you have an unclear sentence, rewrite it from scratch.

- **completeness**
  – Sentence fragments must be corrected. For example,

  Smiling at the camera

  is a fragment, and needs an independent clause to complete it:

  Smiling at the camera, he begun to walk backward to the car

  – Run-ons must be corrected. For example,

  If a person does not exercise a muscle, it will get weak, the same advice applies to the brain.

  is a run-on sentence with a comma splice. It could be rewritten correctly as:

  If a person does not exercise a muscle, it will get weak. The same advice applies to the brain.

- **consistent verb tenses**
  For example,

  We were running, jumped, and slid down the mountain.

  could be changed to one of the following:

  We ran, jumped, and slid down the mountain.

  We were running, jumping, and sliding down the mountain.

- **subject agreement/consistency**
  For example,

  The convict was completely exhausted but kept running because it might still escape.

  should be

  The convict was completely exhausted but kept running because he might still escape.

- **parallel structure in series**

  For example,

  She hoped to finish her essay, that she would print it, and she could hand it in the next day.

  could be changed to

  She hoped to finish her essay, to print it, and to hand it in the next day.

- **variety in sentence types**

  It is boring to read a series of sentences that follow the same formula. For example,

  My cousin says she prefers classical music to pop. She has a large collection of CDs. She never listens to the radio.

  Try the following ways to avoid writing one simple sentence after another:

  – Combine simple sentences to create compound sentences. For example,

  This scene shows both Sybylla and Harry hitting each other with pillows. This also shows Sybylla is interested in Harry.

  could be changed to

  This scene shows Sybylla and Harry hitting each other with pillows, and that Sybylla is interested in Harry.

  – Start the sentence with a transitional word. For example,

  Certainly, the pillow fight scene shows that Sybylla does find Harry interesting.

  – Start the sentence with a clause. For example,

  When Sybylla and Harry are hitting each other with pillows, we see that she is obviously interested in Harry.

  – Start the sentence with a phrase. For example,

  In the pillow-fight scene, it is evident that Sybylla is interested in Harry.

  Be careful here. When a modifier (a word or phrase that limits or describes other words) is too far from what it modifies, the result can be a dangling or misplaced modifier. Check *Modifier* in the Glossary at the end of this book.

Diction

Good diction (choosing the right word) will make your writing clearer. For example, if you are talking about a character's life, it might be more informative to say his life is *tragic* (which has connotations of suffering and misfortune), than to say his life is *sad* (which reduces the suffering considerably).

A thesaurus can be helpful. Use a dictionary to check and confirm that you have chosen the best synonym from the thesaurus. How do you decide which synonym to choose? Consider the following.

Be specific.
Change any general words which are too vague: interesting, different, funny, kind of, etc. For example, *Ralph was afraid of Jack* is not as specific and suggestive of actual meaning as *Ralph was intimidated by Jack*.

Avoid clichés.
Clichés are stale, unoriginal ways of saying something. Examples of clichés to avoid include: the big picture, what goes around, comes around, start from scratch, love of his life, life is like a box of chocolates, get away from it all, food for thought, can't judge a book by its cover, there for me, burned his bridges, face of the earth, etc. Avoid metaphors in essays. Sticking to the literal level is preferable. A better version of, for example, *She was starry-eyed* would be *She was infatuated*.

Avoid euphemisms.
A euphemism is a word or expression that is meant to blunt the impact of unpleasant words or phrases. Some common euphemisms are: *pass away* for *die, rest room* for *washroom*. As a general rule, the direct way is usually best.

Avoid redundancy.
Redundancy is the use of unnecessary words in a sentence: *The reason he speaks in this way is because he is tormented* should be *He speaks in this way because he is tormented*.

Avoid contractions in formal work.
Use words in full. For example, use *do not* instead of *don't*.

Use the correct verb voice.

A verb is in the active voice if its subject is the doer of the action: *The firefighters extinguished the fire.* A verb is in the passive voice (*be* + past participle) when the subject of the verb receives the action: *The fire was extinguished.* The passive voice allows the doer of the action to be omitted. Thus, the doer is unknown, unimportant, or obvious.

Writers of, for example, scientific papers usually prefer the passive voice: *A flame was applied to the mixture.* For writing that is more dynamic, do not use linking verbs. Convert to the active voice, or choose another verb: *I thrust the flaming brand into the brew.*

Avoid *I, you,* and the vague use of *we* or *they*.

Unless you are writing a narrative, a description, or a personal response, keep the I's to a minimum. In most essays, it is not necessary to write *I think* or *in my opinion*, since the essay is your opinion, and a reflection of what you think. You can use personal pronouns to emphasize a personal opinion (*Personally, I felt that the character made the wrong decision for a number of reasons.*) or to identify yourself in a personal response or narrative (*If I had been in that situation, I would have done things differently.*).

The word *you* offers another kind of problem. Writers often try to use it generally (*You'd think people would know better.*). The problem is that the reader may interpret the *you* to mean himself or herself.

We and *they* present similar difficulties. The key question to ask yourself is "Who are *we* or *they*?" There is always a specific answer to that question. For example, if you write *they* in referring to an author, remind yourself that the author is either a male (*he*) or female (*she*). With *we*, ask yourself which *we* is intended: *all of us, people in general, teenagers, Canadians*, or what?

Make sure there is a clear antecedent word for every *he, she, they,* or *it*.

Note the pronoun matchups with the following antecedent words:

Fred — he; the woman — she; people — they; bus — it

The word *it* presents unique problems, but there should be a clear reference to an object (*The door was brightly painted; it was made of wood.*) or something else which is not a person (*Bill was changed by the experience; it made him more suspicious of others.*). The word *this* can often be used as an effective alternative to *it*.

Don't use informal language or slang in formal writing.

Informal language (good guy, ratted on, get tired, plus, sweet) is acceptable in conversations, or in informal writing. Some informal expressions are uniquely meaningful and can be used in formal writing, with quotation marks ("drop out," "become her own person," "dumbing down") as informal expressions for an effect. Use these sparingly.

Slang should always be avoided.

Don't use double negatives.

Using two negative words (for example, *not* and *never*) in the same sentence creates a double negative. Often, these are created in sentences where the word *not* is hidden in a contraction such as *can't*. Avoid confusion by removing or replacing one of the two words: I *can't never get that straight* should be *I can never get that straight*.

A good rule for writers:
Do not explain overmuch.

W. Somerset Maugham

Don't use racist language.

Racist language is any language that refers to a particular cultural or ethnic group in overgeneralized, and often insulting, terms. Here are some ways to avoid racist wording:

- Mention a person's race only if that is relevant to the context:

✗ irrelevant	✓
An Italian man has been charged after a store was deliberately set on fire.	*A man has been charged after a store was deliberately set on fire.*

- If a person's race or ethnic origin is relevant, be as specific as possible:

✗ vague	✓
He emigrated from Asia.	*He emigrated from Beijing, China.*

- Avoid making generalizations about any racial or cultural group:

✗ generalized	✓
The Welsh are great singers.	*The Welsh have a long tradition of singing.*

Don't use sexist language.

Here are some ways to avoid sexist wording:

- Omit *his* or *her* and use *a* or *the*. (*The doctor knows the patient load.*)

- Add *or* if the gender is not clear. (*The doctor knows his or her patient load.*)

- Pluralize the usage. (*Doctors know their patient load.*)

- Look in a thesaurus and substitute non-sexist words.

  Here are a few examples:

✗ non-inclusive	✓ gender-inclusive
man, mankind	human(kind), human beings, humanity, the human race, people
manpower	workers, personnel
workman	worker
chairman, chairwoman	chairperson
policeman	police officer
postman, mailman	mail carrier or letter carrier
fireman	firefighter
steward	flight attendant
weatherman	meteorologist
mothering	parenting

Vocabulary Building

Word choice depends on the vocabulary you have to work with. Talking, reading, and looking up unfamiliar words in a dictionary are important to your development as a writer. You must practise using many words to build up your word bank, in order to communicate more clearly and effectively.

People judge and evaluate others by their language, so the use of weak or inappropriate language in writing — swearing, clichés, slang — may create poor images or impressions. Having a wide palette of words lets you speak, think, write, and communicate at a more mature level.

Here are some suggestions for improving your vocabulary:

- Look up unfamiliar words or terms in a dictionary.
- Read a dictionary, a few pages at a time.
- Read a thesaurus, a few pages at a time.
- Read newspapers and magazines.
- Try word quizzes like those in *Reader's Digest's* "Word Power."
- Try doing crosswords and word searches.
- Read books in areas or genres that truly interest you.
- Browse in bookstores.
- Take notes in class.
- Rewrite assignments, or do extra assignments.
- Talk to friends about movies, and read movie reviews.
- Keep a diary.
- Use e-mail; participate in chat rooms.
- Play word games like Scrabble.
- Write letters (or e-mail) to friends and family members.

*Our words must seem
to be inevitable.*

William Butler Yeats

Using a Thesaurus

A thesaurus provides many synonyms for common words which might otherwise be overused.

Take, for instance, the vague word *interesting*. A thesaurus provides these alternate choices: *absorbing, compelling, engaging, gripping* (and many more). These words are clearer, sharper, and more specific in meaning.

Be wary, however, of using a thesaurus to drop fancy polysyllabic words into your writing. For example, you could replace the word *fun* with the word *jocularity*, in an attempt to impress. Your writing (and you) will probably just look foolish. It is better to spend your time trying to clarify your thoughts. Focus on clear, honest communication.

*All good writing is
swimming under water and
holding your breath.*

F. Scott Fitzgerald

COMMONLY CONFUSED WORDS

A/An

A is used before nouns starting with consonants.
*Ravi had **a** dream of becoming successful.*

An is used before nouns starting with vowels.
*Susan ate **an** apple.*

Accept/Except

Accept is a verb meaning receive.
*The actor will **accept** the award from the academy.*

Except is usually a preposition meaning *other than.*
*Everyone **except** John is going to university.*

Advice/Advise

Advice is a noun.
*The talk show host gave **advice** about relationships to newlyweds.*

Advise is a verb.
*The government will **advise** students of their marks on diploma exams.*

Affect/Effect

Affect is most often a verb meaning *influence.*
*The hospital closure will adversely **affect** the community.*

Effect is usually a noun meaning *result.*
*Television can have the **effect** of making people more materialistic.*

Aggravate/Irritate

Aggravate in formal English means *make worse.*
*Scratching a mosquito bite will **aggravate** the swelling.*

Irritate means *annoy.*
*That mosquito is **irritating** me.*

Allude/Refer

Allude means *make an indirect reference.*
*That remark about trees **alluded** to the incident at the picnic.*

Refer means *make a direct reference.*
*He **referred** to the play's second act in order to make his point.*

Allusion/Illusion

Allusion means *reference to something well-known.*
> On The Simpsons, *there was an* **allusion** *to Edgar Allan Poe's famous poem "The Raven."*

Illusion means *false idea.*
> *The mirage created the* **illusion** *of water on the desert horizon.*

Alot/A lot

Alot is a misspelling of the correct *a lot.*

Already/All ready

Already is an adjective meaning *by this time.*
> *It is* **already** *too late in the day to go to the beach.*

All ready is an adverb meaning *completely ready.*
> *The sprinter was* **all ready** *for her track event.*

Alright/All right

Alright is the informal spelling of *all right.*
It should be avoided in formal writing.

All right remains the preferred spelling.
> *All the drivers in the accident were* **all right**.

Altogether/All together

Altogether means *completely* or *all things considered.*
> **Altogether**, *there were four touchdowns in the football game.*

All together emphasizes all things in a group.
> *The classroom teachers brought the students* **all together** *in the gym.*

Among/Between

Among implies more than two people or things.
> *There are many celebrities scattered* **among** *the large crowd.*

Between refers to only two in number.
> *Jameel and I split the chips* **between** *us.*

Amount/Number

Amount is used to refer to something in a mass.
> *We ordered a large* **amount** *of topsoil for the garden.*

Number is used to refer to individual, countable items.
> *We ordered a large* **number** *of plants for the garden.*

A part of/Apart from

A part of means *a member of, a section of,* or *a piece of.*
A part of the airplane fell from the sky.

Apart from means *separate* or *isolated from.*
Martin Luther King was a man of integrity who stood **apart** from the crowd.

Assure/Ensure/Insure

Assure means *restore confidence.*
The doctor will **assure** you that you are healthy.

Ensure means *make certain or safe.*
A bank safe deposit box can **ensure** the safety of your jewellery.

Insure means *arrange payment to cover loss.*
You ought to **insure** your house, car, and other valuables.

Bear/Bare

Bear is either a noun referring to a large furry mammal, or a verb meaning *put up with.*
Facing a grizzly **bear** so soon after a cougar attack was more than I could **bear**.

Bare is often an adjective meaning *uncovered, naked,* or *empty.*
Bare skin freezes quickly in the arctic conditions of **bare** tundra.

Beside/Besides

Beside means *by the side of.*
The grass **beside** the fence needs cutting.

Besides means *in addition to.*
Who is coming **besides** us?

Board/Bored

Board is usually a noun referring to wood, a group of people, or a chalkboard.
Each school **board** member wrote his or her name on the bulletin **board**.

Bored is the past tense of the verb *bore,* and means *tired* or *uninterested.*
After watching fast-paced, noisy, animated cartoons, kindergarten pupils may be **bored** listening to someone talking at the front of a classroom.

Break/Brake

Break is most often used as a verb meaning *damage* or as a noun meaning *pause* or *welcome change in activity.*
*The child will likely **break** the toy if he continues to play with it roughly.*
*The professor gave her class a coffee **break** to discuss the upcoming spring **break**.*

Brake is commonly used in its noun form, referring to a tool or machine part for stopping the motion of a moving object.
*Step lightly on your car **brake** when appoaching an intersection.*

Breath/Breathe

Breath is a noun.
*Take a deep **breath**.*

Breathe is a verb.
***Breathe** normally while the doctor checks your chest.*

Burned/Burnt

Although these terms are often used interchangeably, *burned* is more formal, *burnt* more informal.
Burned is frequently used as a verb.
*The child **burned** herself on the hot stove.*

Burnt is more likely to be used as an adjective.
*Most meat-eaters do not prefer to eat **burnt** steak.*

Buy/By

Buy is a verb meaning *purchase.*
*When you start your first job, you can **buy** your own clothes.*

By is a preposition meaning *beside* or *through the act of.*
*He was standing **by** the car pumping gas.*
Citizen Kane, *directed **by** Orson Welles, is considered by many critics to be the greatest American film.*

Can/May

Can means *able to.*
*People **can** do anything they put their minds to.*

May suggests possibility, opportunity, or permission.
***May** I leave the table? It **may** rain later today.*

Cannot/Can not

Both verbs are acceptable, although *cannot* reflects common pronunciation.

However, *can not* is preferred for emphasizing the negative.

The Canadian government **cannot** *seem to solve the problem of unemployment.*

I **can not** *swim no matter how hard I try.*

Child/Kid

Child is the preferred formal version of the informal, sometimes derogatory *kid*.

They adopted a **child** *for humanitarian reasons.*

Natasha was just a **kid** *in so many ways.*

Childish/Childlike

Childish means *immature like a child*, and has negative connotations when applied to an adult.

The man was **childish** *in his attitude and behaviour.*

Childlike means *innocent like a child*, and has positive connotations when applied to an adult.

The man had a **childlike** *respect for his elderly parents.*

Choose/Chose/Choice

These three terms are often confused in pronunciation and spelling.

Choose is a present tense verb, *chose* is a past tense verb, *choice* is a noun.

Choose *your partner carefully.*

I **chose** *to finish the course.*

Ngaio had to make a difficult **choice**.

Conscience/Conscious

Conscience is a noun meaning *awareness of right or wrong*.

The criminal had no **conscience** *about his crimes.*

Conscious is an adjective meaning *aware*.

Michelle was not **conscious** *of her friend's jealous nature.*

Could of/Could have

Could of is the informal, conversational form of the formally correct *could have*.

Jaswant **could have** *e-mailed her cousin in India.*

Couple/Few/Several

Couple always refers to two in number.
*A **couple** of months went by before their subscription expired.*

Few may refer specifically to three, or not many more than that.
*A **few** players did not like their hot-tempered coach.*

Several usually refers to more than a few, but not many, e.g., from four to seven.
*I chose **several** books from the library.*

Course/Coarse

Course is a noun meaning *series of studies,* or *direction taken.*
*We found the calculus **course** challenging.*

Coarse is an adjective meaning *rough* or *crude.*
*Some of the passengers used **coarse** language which upset the parents of young children aboard.*

Credible/Credulous/Creditable

Credible means *capable of being believed.*
*A lie can be **credible**.*

Credulous means *willing to believe.*
*He remained **credulous**, even when we told ridiculous lies.*

Creditable means *worthy of being believed.*
*A lie should not be **creditable**.*

Disinterested/Uninterested

Disinterested means *neutral and fair.*
*A **disinterested** onlooker agreed to referee the game.*

Uninterested means *not interested.*
*She was **uninterested** in watching the movie.*

Due to/Because of

Due to refers to schedules and timelines.
*The train is **due to** arrive before midnight.*

Because of is the more formal general expression meaning *as a result of.*
***Because of** his broken collarbone, he missed a few weeks of school.*

Etc./Ect./And so forth

Etc., written in full as the Latin *et cetera* (two words), means *and so forth*.

Etc. is usually used only in business writing; otherwise, a writer would write *and so forth* for general formal usage.
> *People are likely to judge others on their appearance, language, attitudes, actions,* **and so forth**.

Ect. is an incorrect spelling of *etc*.
> *The office contained monitors, hard drives, printers, modems, fax machines,* **etc.**

Everyone/Every one

Everyone is the general expression, except when emphasis is desired; in that case, *every one* is used.
> **Everyone** *is going to the dance tonight.*
> **Every one** *of us is expected to make an individual contribution.*

Farther/Further

Although these terms are used interchangeably, *farther* refers to physical distance, while *further* relates to general amount or quantity.
> *They skied* **farther** *down the mountain than they ever had before.*
> *He took* **further** *action on the complaint.*

Fewer/Less

Fewer refers to things which can be counted or itemized.
> *There were* **fewer** *voters than the last election.*

Less refers to general amounts.
> *Edmonton receives* **less** *snow than Winnipeg.*

Funny/Strange

Funny is used as an informal term meaning *odd* or *strange*. But strictly speaking, *funny* refers to something which is hilarious or laughable.
> *Charlie Chaplin is one of the best-known* **funny** *men of film.*

Strange is a more limited term referring to the unfamiliar or unnatural.
> *His close encounter of the third kind was a* **strange** *experience.*

Good/Well

Good is an adjective.
> *Is this a* **good** *way to go?*

Well is an adverb.
> *You write* **well**.

Great/Grate

Great is a commonly used adjective meaning *large* or *important.*
> *Mother Teresa and Terry Fox are examples of* **great** *humanitarians who did remarkable things for others.*

Grate is used as a noun referring to a framework of iron bars used in fires, or as a verb (with *on*) meaning *wear down* or *annoy.*
> *The* **grate** *in the fireplace will* **grate** *on your ears if it is dragged across the bricks.*

Here/Hear

Here is used as an adverb or subject and means *in this place.*
> **Here** *are several reasons for courtesy.*
> *The dog came* **here** *and sat down.*

Hear is a verb referring to the act of listening.
> *Do you* **hear** *the sound of marching feet?*

Hole/Whole

The more common word *hole* refers to an opening or hollow.
> *Alice followed the rabbit down his* **hole***.*

Whole means *complete,* or *entire thing.*
> *I ate the* **whole** *pie!*

Imply/Infer

Imply means *suggest.*
> *Her expression* **implied** *that she disagreed with me.*

Infer means *draw a conclusion.*
> *I* **inferred** *from her smile that she was happy.*

It's/Its

It's is a contraction of *it is* or *it has.*
> **It's** *a lesson too late for the learning.*

Its is a possessive pronoun.
> *Look at the dog — it's got my shoe in* **its** *mouth.*

Knew/New

Knew is a verb meaning *was familiar with* or *had knowledge of.*
> *Kajtek* **knew** *the quickest way to get to our house.*

New is an adjective meaning *never before used.*
> *The* **new** *cars had arrived at the showroom.*

Later/Latter/Former

Later refers to time.
> *The buses were running **later** than usual.*

Latter refers to the last-mentioned item; *former* to the first or previously mentioned.
> *Kennedy and Nixon were both American presidents; the **former** was assassinated and the **latter** resigned after the Watergate scandal.*

Lay/Lie/Laid/Lain

Writers should not confuse the two separate verb conjugations: *lie-lay-lain* are intransitive verbs (lacking objects) meaning *recline*.
> *The poodle owner told Pepper to **lie** down.*
> *He **lay** down in the shade under the trees.*
> *The cat has **lain** around the house looking ill.*

Lay-laid-laid are transitive verbs meaning *set in place*.
> ***Lay** down your weapons.*
> *We **laid** the rumour to rest.*
> *This is the goose that has **laid** the golden egg.*

Lead/Led

Lead can be used as a verb (pronounced *leed*) meaning guide, or as a noun (pronounced *led*) meaning a kind of metal.
> *You can **lead** a horse to water but you can't make it drink.*
> *Consumption of **lead** can be toxic.*

Led is the past tense of the verb to lead.
> *The team was **led** by its captain.*

Learned/Learnt/Teach

Although these terms are often used interchangeably, *learned* is more formal, *learnt* more informal.
Learned is frequently used as a verb.
> *In social studies, we **learned** about many types of government.*

Learnt is more likely to be used as an adjective.
> *Language arts includes the **learnt** skills of listening, viewing, and representing.*

Teach means *present lessons*.
> ***Teach** me how to fly.*

Leave/Let

Leave is often used as a verb meaning *go away*, or *give*.
> ***Leave** at your own chosen speed.*

Let is a verb meaning *allow*.
> *It's said to be best to **let** sleeping dogs lie.*

Like/As/Similar to

Like can be used as a preposition, *as* can be used as an adverb, and *similar to* is a more formal phrasing of *like*.
Like a bridge over troubled waters, I will lay me down.
*The pony ran **as** fast **as** the wind.*
*The daughters were **similar to** their mother in physical appearance.*

Loan/Borrow

Loan can be used as a verb meaning *allow (someone the use of),* or as a noun meaning *payment,* or *something borrowed.*
*The library can **loan** us books to take out, but not magazines.*
*The bank branch gave us a **loan** on our mortgage.*

Borrow is a verb meaning *use (someone else's property or money).*
*May I **borrow** your extra pen?*

Lose/Loose/Loss

These three words are often mispronounced and misspelled.
Lose (pronounced like *looz*) is a verb meaning *be defeated.*
*We have to learn how to **lose** graciously.*

Loose (pronounced like *looss*) is an adjective meaning *not contained.*
*Do you have any **loose** change?*
*Don't let **loose** the alligator.*

Loss (pronounced like *lawce*) is a noun referring to a defeat.
*How did the home team take the **loss**?*

Mad/Angry/Insane

Mad can mean both *upset and annoyed* (more general and informal) and *insane* (reflecting more of the original meaning).
*The stress of modern living can cause one to go **mad**.*
*Lady Macbeth became increasingly **mad** from guilt after she assisted in a murder.*

Angry is a more specific, formal way of saying *upset* or *furious.*
*I was very **angry** and disappointed with him.*

Man/Guy

Man is more formal than the informal *guy*, which may even be derogatory.
*The **man** was definitely a hero.*
*He was just some **guy** she met.*

No-one/No one

No-one is a much less commonly used, though acceptable, hyphenated form of *no one*.
> **No one** *will know if you don't want them to.*

Off of/Off

Off of is an extremely informal expression for *off*. Do not use it in writing.
> *The fork fell* **off** *the table.*

OK/O.K./Okay

These are informal expressions for the more formal *all right*.
> *Is it* **OK** *to leave early?*

Passed/Past

Passed is a past tense verb.
> *The car* **passed** *us on the highway.*

Past is used as a noun, adjective, or preposition.
> *The* **past** *comes well before the future.*
> *Her* **past** *life caught up with her.*
> *He drove* **past** *the exit.*

Patience/Patients

Patience is usually a desirable character quality.
> **Patience** *is a virtue when you have to sit in a waiting room.*

Patients are people who have a doctor.
> *The doctor had many* **patients** *who trusted her.*

Payed/Paid

Payed is a misspelling of *paid*.
> *The manager* **paid** *the employee.*

Phase/Faze

Phase is a noun meaning *period* or *spell*.
> *Depression is a* **phase** *many people experience.*

Faze is an informal verb meaning *bother* or *upset*.
> *Nothing could* **faze** *the concentration of the figure-skater.*

Piece/Peace

Piece refers to a section or portion.
> *Please give me a* **piece** *of chocolate cake.*

Peace refers to quiet, or a state of non-war.
> *He knew no* **peace** *after his secret identity had been discovered.*

Plane/Plain

Plane is a noun most often describing a shortened spelling for *airplane*.
> The **plane** circled the airport before landing.

Plain is used as an adjective to mean *obvious, ordinary-looking,* or *simple*.
> It was **plain** that the man was **plain**-looking.

Plus/&/And

Plus and *&* should be used only in mathematics, or in informal writing.
Writers sometimes make the mistake of using *plus* at the beginning of a sentence to mean *also*.
> The wind **and** cold temperatures created hazardous driving conditions.
> **Also**, the road had dangerous black ice on it.

Principal/Principle

Principal can be used as a noun meaning *head of a school* or as an adjective meaning *main*.
> Mrs. Brown, the **principal**, is the **principal** reason why this school is successful.

Principle is a noun which refers to fundamental belief.
> Honesty is a guiding **principle** in his life.

Prejudice/Prejudism

There is no such word as *prejudism*. The correct word is *prejudice*, which means *the state of prejudging others or something before getting to know them/it well*.
> We need to set aside our own **prejudice** in order to become more tolerant and understanding.

Proceed/Precede

Proceed means *go ahead*.
> **Proceed** to the gym for the assembly.

Precede means *come before*.
> The police motorcycle will **precede** the prime minister's motorcade.

Quite/Quiet/Quit

Quite is an adjective meaning *really, completely, actually,* or *positively*.
> Shireen was **quite** upset by his snub.

Quiet is an adjective meaning *still, peaceful, without noise*.
> Try to be **quiet** in a library.

Quit is a verb meaning *stop* or *leave*.
> The losing candidate **quit** his campaign and then **quit** the party.

Raise/Rise

Raise means *lift up*.
> *There was a plan to **raise** the* Titanic.

Rise means *get up*.
> *Are you early to **rise** in the morning?*

Real/Really

In formal usage, *real* is an adjective and *really* is an adverb.
> *What's the **real** story on this cover-up?*
> *I swam **really** well in the final.*

Regardless/Irregardless

There is no such word as *irregardless*. The correct word is *regardless*, which means *in any case* or *in spite of*.
> *They went cycling **regardless** of the bad weather.*

Role/Roll

Role is a noun which refers to a part played.
> *What **role** did he play in her life?*

Roll is often used as a verb meaning *turn over*, or as a noun referring to a bread food.
> ***Roll** the ball to me.*
> *Do I get a **roll** with my soup?*

Saw/Seen

Seen is sometimes used interchangeably and wrongly with *saw*, as in *I seen the two movies*. (Note, though, that *seen* can be correct when used with the auxiliary verbs *have* or *had*.)
> *I **saw** the two movies.*
> *I **have seen** the two movies.*

Set/Sit

Things are *set* (a verb indicating placement and arrangement).
> *The table was **set** for twelve diners.*

People and things can *sit* (a verb meaning *rest on the buttocks*).
> ***Sit** down and make yourself at home.*

Should of/Should have

Should of is the informal conversational pronunciation of the formally correct *should have*.
> *I **should have** known better.*

Sight/Site/Cite

As a noun or verb, the more common *sight* refers to something seen, whereas the noun *site* refers to place or centre.
> *After he fell in the mud, he was quite a **sight**.*
> *Did you **sight** the U.F.O.?*
> *The band set up a **Web site** on the Internet.*

Cite is a verb meaning *indicate a reference*.
> *Did you **cite** your references in your essay?*

Sneaked/Snuck

Snuck is the informal, conversational version of *sneaked*.
> *The child **sneaked** a cookie while no one was looking.*

Soul/Sole

Soul is a noun that refers to spirit.
> *Claudius's **soul** was ensnared in guilt.*

Sole is an adjective meaning *only*, or a noun referring to a type of fish.
> *The **sole** reason for my not ordering the **sole** is that I don't like fish.*

Sure/Surely

Sure is an adjective meaning *certain* or *definite*.
> *The police were not **sure** of his innocence.*

Surely is an adverb meaning *certainly* or *without fail*.
> ***Surely** the jury will see through the lies of the accused.*

Than/Then

Than is used for comparison.
> *Surprisingly, the girl gymnast was more agile **than** her older competitors.*

Then is an adverb meaning *at that time*, or *soon afterward*.
> ***Then** he came to a new understanding about himself.*

That/Which/Who

That can refer generally to both persons or things.
> *The people **that** were in the elevator were trapped for hours.*

Which refers specifically to things.
> *The voting rights of the people, **which** are guaranteed by law, make democracy work well.*

Who refers specifically to persons.
> *She was the woman **who** had her purse stolen.*

There/Their/They're

There is an adverb meaning *at that place*.
Go **there**.

Their is a possessive pronoun meaning *belonging to them*.
We saw the Singhs at **their** house.

They're is a contraction for *they are*.
They're always right.

Through/Threw

Through is used as a preposition meaning *from one side to another, over,* or *by means of*.
The rock crashed **through** the window.
The executive went **through** his aerobic exercises.

Threw is the past tense of the verb *throw* which means *toss* or *hurl*.
The pitcher **threw** the ball to the catcher.

Till/Until

These interchangeable words mean the same thing.
Till is more informal.
The floodwaters kept rising **till** the banks gave way.

Until is preferred at the beginnings of sentences.
Until she finished high school, she never had a regular job.

To/Too/Two

To is most often a preposition meaning *in the direction of*.
They went **to** the folk festival.

Too is an adverb meaning *also* or *more than enough*.
I'm going, **too**. There are **too** many weeds on the lawn.

Two is the word for the numeral 2.
Two players were traded before the deadline.

Uninterested/Disinterested

Uninterested refers to being bored or not paying attention.
The six year-old boy was **uninterested** in the love story.

Disinterested refers to having a neutral interest or being impersonal.
A referee is supposed to be **disinterested** in the outcome of the game.

Use to/Used to

Use to is a mispronounced informal usage for the grammatically correct *used to*.
He **used to** play in the tree fort.

Where/Wear

Where is an adverb meaning *in (at/to/from) what place.*
Where *are you going?*

Wear is a verb meaning *put on the body,* or a noun and verb
both referring to damage done to something.
What should we **wear** *to the commencement ceremony?*
The back tires were showing signs of **wear**.

Whether/Weather

Whether is a conjunction suggesting choice and is often
followed by *or not.*
She did not know **whether** *or not to make a donation to this*
charity.

Weather is a noun referring to atmospheric conditions.
We watch the **weather** *carefully when we are sailing.*

Which/Witch

Which is the more common word; it is a pronoun used to ask
questions.
Which *route are you taking to get to the mountains?*

Witch is a noun referring to a woman supposed to have
magic powers.
On Halloween, my sister dressed up as a **witch**.

Who's/Whose

Who's is a contraction which means *who is* or *who has.*
Who's *on my side?* **Who's** *got the puck?*

Whose is a possessive pronoun expressing ownership.
Whose *life is it anyway?*

Would of/Would have

Similar to *could of* and *should of,* *would of* is an informal,
conversational version of the formally correct *would have.*
We **would have** *attended the concert if we had known how good it*
was going to be.

You're/Your

You're is a contraction for *you are.*
You're *just the person we're looking for.*

Your is a possessive pronoun meaning *belonging to you.*
Your *dog wants to go for a walk.*

Spelling

Having correct spelling is a matter of accuracy and, like any other writing skill, takes practice. In the sections that follow, you will find basic spelling rules, hints for problem spellers, and a list of commonly misspelled words.

Basic Spelling Rules

Here are some basic spelling rules that are well worth knowing:

To change singular nouns to plural:

Add *s: bird — birds*

For words ending in *s*, add *es*: bus — buses

To change verb tenses in verbs ending with *y*:

Drop the *y* and add *ies: carry — carries*

Use *i* before *e* except after *c*:

sieve, brief, chief, believe, yield, grief, thief, friend

receive, perceive, receipt, conceive, deceive

Here are some exceptions which you should memorize:

being, foreign, leisure, neighbour, their, vein, weigh, weight, weird

Some words have silent letters:

subtle, autumn, column, palm

Double such consonants as *n*, *p*, etc., before *-ed* or *-ing* suffixes:

beginning, shopped, occurring, permitted

Drop the *e* before *-able* suffixes:

valuable, excitable, lovable

Here are some exceptions to remember:

noticeable, changeable

Spelling Tips

Break words up into syllables:

> *con-cern-ing, dif-fer-ent, hand-ker-chief, in-ter-est, mo-ti-va-tion*

Mentally set off prefixes and suffixes from the rest of the word:

> *avail-able, de-scribe, lov-ing, pre-view, watch-ed*

Use memory cues based on "buried words" within a longer word:

> *bus*i*ness, sepa*ra*te, tempe*ra*ture*

Keep a notebook section of spelling errors from old assignments:

> Make two columns. Put the error in the left-hand column, then make the correction on the right. Use this to memorize words that you often misspell. Also, review these same pages while you're working on an assignment, or before a test.

Use a spell checker:

> Most computers have spell-check functions. If you don't have access to a computer, consider getting a portable spell checker, which is relatively inexpensive and acceptable for use in many classrooms. It gives the correct spellings for words you can only "sound-spell":
>
> fashin → fashion
>
> bizness → business

Use a dictionary:

> A spell checker *can't* pick out the correct homophone for a specific context. Using the search function to identify homophones may be helpful, but you must follow up by using a dictionary. There are many homophones in English: bare/bear, board/bored, cite/sight, dear/deer, grate/great, hole/whole, lead/led, meat/meet, peace/piece, right/write, threw/through, way/weigh, and so on.

Test yourself:

> On the following pages you will find a list of commonly misspelled words. Have a friend or family member dictate these words to you, and write them down.

Commonly Misspelled Words

Here is a list of words commonly misspelled by high school students. Test yourself until you get all (or most) of the words right.

The spelling of these words is the preferred version given in the *Gage Canadian Dictionary*, with alternate spellings given after.

absence	amateur	boundary
absorption	among	breathe
accessory	analyse	brilliant
accidentally	*or* analyze	brochure
accommodation	analysis	business
accompanying	answered	calendar
accumulate	anxious	campaign
achieve	apologize	catalogue
acknowledgment	apparent	*or* catalog
or acknowledgement	appearance	category
acquaintance	appropriate	certain
acquire	argument	character
acquisition	article	cheque
across	assistance	*or* check
actually	athletics	chief
address	attendance	children
adjacent	author	chronological
adolescence	autumn	clothes
advantageous	available	coincidence
advertisement	barely	collage
adviser	basically	college
or advisor	beginning	colonel
advisory	behaviour	column
affiliated	*or* behavior	commitment
against	believe	committee
aggressive	benefit	compatible
alleged	biassed	completely
all right	*or* biased	concede

condemn
conscience
conscientious
conscious
consensus
contradiction
convenience
correspondent
courageous
courtesy
cried
criticism
curiosity
debt
decision
definitely
describe
desirable
desperately
destroy
development
different
dilemma
disappointed
disastrous
discipline
doesn't
dying
eighth
eligible
eliminate
embarrassed
emphasize
entrepreneur
environment

escape
especially
eventually
exaggerate
excellence
exercise
existence
experience
extraordinary
extremely
fallacy
familiar
fascinating
February
finally
flexible
foreign
foresee
foreshadowing
fortunate
forty
fulfil
  or fulfill
gesture
goddess
government
grammar
guarantee
  or guaranty
handkerchief
harassment
heroes
honourable
  or honorable
humorous

illegible
immediately
incidentally
incredible
independent
inevitable
innuendo
insistent
instalment
  or installment
intelligent
interesting
interfere
irrelevant
irresistible
jealous
jeopardy
jewellery
  or jewelry
judgment
  or judgement
knowledgeable
  or knowledgable
laid
leisure
liar
library
likable
  or likeable
literature
loneliness
losing
manner
marriage
married

meant
miniature
miscellaneous
mischievous
misspell
mortgage
naive
necessary
neighbour
  or neighbor
niece
ninety
ninth
no one
  or no-one
noticeable
nowadays
nuclear
occasion
occurrence
offence
  or offense
omission
opinion
optimistic
paid
parallel
paralyse
  or paralyze
parliament
particular
pastime
peculiar
perseverance
persistence

personal
personnel
persuade
phenomenal
piece
plagiarism
playwright
portrays
possession
preceding
preferable
preferred
prejudice
presence
presumptuous
pretence
  or pretense
previously
privilege
probably
procedure
proceed
professor
psychology
pursue
questionnaire
realistically
realize
receipt
receive
recommend
referring
reinforce
related
relevant

remembrance
resemblance
restaurant
rhyme
rhythm
Saskatchewan
schedule
science
scissors
seize
sense
separate
Shakespeare
similar
sincerely
skilful
  or skillful
soldier
soliloquy
souvenir
speech
spirited
stereotype
straight
strength
subconscious
subtle
succeed
summary
supposed
surprise
suspense
technique
temperamental
temperature

tempt	tries	vicious
tendency	truly	view
theatre	Tuesday	villain
or theater	ultimately	Wednesday
theory	unconscious	weird
therefore	undoubtedly	wherever
thoroughly	unfortunately	whole
together	unique	writer
tomorrow	unnecessary	writing
tragedy	usage	yield
tragic	usually	
transferred	vacuum	
traveller	vegetable	
or traveler	vehicle	

What is not recorded
is not remembered.

Benazir Bhutto

Punctuation

In spoken English, you can use different tones of voice, pauses, and volume changes to make your meaning clear. In writing, your only tool is marks on paper. Correct punctuation is essential.

Apostrophe

This punctuation mark is used for two main functions:

1. in a contraction, to indicate missing letters:

   you are → you're

2. in a possessive, to indicate ownership:

   the shirt that belongs to Bill → Bill's shirt

- A single owner is written as *'s*, while plural owners are indicated by *s'*:

   Elena's rollerblades (one Elena), *the Smiths' house* (more than one Smith)

- Some writers prefer to write *s's* for the possessive of names ending in *s*:

   Charles Dickens's book (pronounced Dickenzez) although *Dickens' book* is also correct.

- How can you tell when a possessive apostrophe is needed? There will be two nouns side by side:

   Frank's car, my sister's bike

- A common mistake is to assume that every word ending in *s* needs an apostrophe even if the word is not a contraction, or is not being used in a possessive. The following is **incorrect**:

   The concert's were both excellently staged.

   Look carefully and ask yourself if letters are missing. Ask yourself what belongs to the concert — nothing. So, the apostrophe is not needed.

- Some words form irregular plurals that do not end in *s*. Therefore, you do not add *s'* to these:

   men's shoes, women's clothing, children's toys

- A common mistake is to use *it's* instead of *its*, and vice versa.

  The contraction is *it's*, (*it is*, or *it has*) and always has an apostrophe:

  It's a nice day.

  The possessive is *its*, (belonging to *it*) and never has an apostrophe:

  The dog has chewed its basket.

Colon

Colons (:) are used in three common ways:

- Before a list:

  We added the following ingredients: flour, eggs, and milk.

- Before an elaboration of a point or idea:

  The author expresses the following point: people cannot be trusted.

- Before a quotation:

  Hamlet shows his willingness to die when he says to Horatio: "The readiness is all."

Comma

Commas (,) are used in several ways:

- To punctuate a series:

  Colin, Coty, and Alice are flying to Toronto.

  Note that the comma before *and* is optional.

- To set off a transitional word, phrase, or clause at the beginning of a sentence:

  In fact, we won.

  Walking round the garden, Shalah stared up at the moon.

  When I have a birthday, I get a lot of cards.

- To set off additional or supportive information from the rest of a sentence:

  Hamlet, Gertrude's son, is melancholy.

- Before co-ordinate conjunctions (*and, but, yet*):

  The Canadiens won the game, but lost the series.

Commas create pauses when a sentence is read, so try to place your commas so that they do not unnecessarily interrupt the flow of the sentence.

If in doubt, omit the comma.

Dash

Dashes (—) are used to separate sidetracking or contrasting information from the rest of a sentence.

The piece of metal — which everyone had completely forgotten about — got stuck in the gearshift.

Ellipsis Points

Ellipsis points . . . are used to indicate that words have been omitted from a quotation. Some style guides prefer square brackets around the points:

He was a good parent [. . .] his methods showed patience.

End Punctuation

A sentence will end with a period, a question mark, or an exclamation mark.

- Use a period at the end of a statement:

  I have to catch that bus.

- In some statements, you may want to register strong emotion. Use an exclamation mark:

  I must catch that bus!

- If the sentence is a question, use a question mark.

  Why do you have to catch that bus?

As a rule, only one end punctuation mark is used in formal and most creative writing. Don't use punctuation in a distracting manner, as the following example does: *Do you know you made me miss that bus!!??!!*

Hyphen

Hyphens (-) are used mainly as follows.

- in some compound words:

    well-spoken, fast-moving, well-being

- to link connected words:

    easy-to-use, paint-by-numbers

- between numbers:

    twenty-nine, four-sevenths

- with some prefixes:

    anti-American, ex-student, semi-intelligent

Parentheses

Parentheses ( ) are used to add extra information, in order to elaborate or make something clearer:

Lachlan hated dogs. (As a child he had been bitten at a dog show.)

This effect should only be used up to a few times in an essay; otherwise, the effect gives an unfinished, unpolished appearance.

Quotation Marks

- Quotation marks (" ") are mainly used to indicate the words someone has said:

    "To be or not to be" are the opening words of Hamlet's most famous speech.

- Single quotation marks are used to indicate a quotation within a quotation:

    Janet said, "'To be or not to be' is the opening of Hamlet's most famous speech."

- The titles of brief works of literature (poems, short stories, and essays) are given in quotation marks:

    "Boys and Girls"

Semicolon

Semicolons (;) are used to separate two or more independent clauses that relate closely to each other:

Jovan knew his limitations; he knew when to quit.

If the two clauses are not closely related, use a period:

She moved to Victoria. Her mother told her that winters were mild there.

Square Brackets

Square brackets [ ] are used when omitting words, or substituting words for others, especially in quotations:

The critic said that [Macbeth] knew he was doomed when he heard that Dunsinane Wood was coming to his castle.

The original words were *the king.*

If you wish to be a writer, write.

Epictetus

Capitalization

Capital letters are used:

- as the first letter on the first word at the beginning of a sentence.

- as the first letter of a name or a language.

- in titles, for the first letters of the first and last words as well as the nouns and verbs:

  One Flew over the Cuckoo's Nest

Titles

Basic rules to remember for quoting titles are:

- Use quotation marks for anything brief, or which comes from a full-length work. This includes short stories, short poems, essays, articles, short films:

  "The Road Not Taken"

- Use italics (or underlining when writing by hand) for longer works. This includes newspapers, magazines, books, or feature films:

  The Globe and Mail, Maclean's, Death of a Salesman, Jurassic Park

Writing Numbers

Styles vary, but usually:

- Numbers less than three digits are written out in full:

  five, forty

- Numbers of three or more digits are represented by numbers:

  100, 2001

- Fractions are generally written in full:

  one-half

- Numbers written as adjectives or adverbs are generally written in full:

  first, nineteenth

Writing Skills Practice Exercises

Review the examples provided in the following practice exercises to identify the common writing errors.

Sentence Errors

(For more information on sentences, see pp. 117-118.)

1. Doubling to ensure your safety.

2. When my family has reunions.

3. When she felt lonely, she would write, in fact writing was her salvation.

4. They become more than roommates, they become brothers.

5. Paul breaks away from his father's technique. While Norman and the father keep casting the traditional way.

6. Conrad makes good progress. Which is what makes it possible for him to survive his depression.

7. Swarn is friendly and kind, he has been very helpful to us.

8. Running down the road.

9. He was friendly. He was also kind. He was decent, too.

10. There are other ways to solve problems. Like discussing matters over tea.

11. The horse reared, was whinnying, and had bolted for the pasture.

12. The dog chased the possum along the fence until they caught the poor creature.

13. The shortstop fielded the baseball, could bobble it, and would relay it to first.

14. I am the last person to ask for tax advice, I cannot even correctly add a column of numbers.

15. He is a competent painter, but when he tries.

(For answers, see p. 166.)

Agreement Problems

(For more information on agreement, see pp. 121, 184-185,187.)

1. She is welcome to bring their own car.

2. Macbeth, not his wife, are plotting to kill King Duncan.

3. Anybody who want to start is welcome to do so.

4. She is a powerful women.

5. Maggie liked to swim, riding, and tennis.

6. Dustin, together with Richard and Omar, were given raises.

7. A pencil and a ruler is a useful tool.

8. The team is up for the game; they might win.

9. One should remember to phone his parents.

10. The whole family are upset.

11. When the average Canadian complains about taxes, they say that no one cares.

12. Although a pocket thesaurus is useful, they cannot replace a standard desk thesaurus.

13. The bug's antennae is severely bent.

14. A list of the required books, along with the timetable, are included.

15. The whole committee are infuriated.

(For answers, see p. 167.)

Word Choice

(For more information about word choice, see pp. 119-125.)

1. I went to see the doctor due to my bad cold.

2. He was the guy who lost his mutt.

3. When one looks beneath the surface of the poem, I can see that the author or the speaker is concerned with death.

4. She cracks.

5. She changes her mind; she would have wanted a career.

6. Maybe the boy isn't getting attention they need.

7. The poppies are a new flower.

8. This movie sucks.

9. Hitler was a sort of evil man.

10. The boy's comment could of revealed prejudice.

11. You can see the comedian's mug in every newspaper across Canada.

12. The detergent is the best cleanser known to man.

13. Victoria has fewer rain than Prince Rupert.

14. If you master all the components of the program, you will certainly be able to write good.

15. The pipes that are in the garage need to be organized according to size.

(For answers, see p. 167.)

Homophones

(For more information about homophones, see pp. 126-142.)

1. There was no one there accept the staff.

2. Are you all ready finished?

3. He was under the allusion that he was earning twenty-five dollars an hour.

4. Their coming inside with there umbrellas.

5. He couldn't bare to leave his family for long.

6. Romar was on bored the plane by one o'clock.

7. The old car was a site for soar eyes.

8. Did you ever here of anything so absurd?

9. Your certain?

10. Before you buy you're new car, you should get the insurance.

11. Who is the principle of you're school?

12. As a basketball guard, she has no pier.

13. In the provincial museum, one is not aloud to shout.

14. The Queen has witnessed many changes in Canada during her rain.

15. The loan robber made her getaway from the bank.

(For answers, see p. 168.)

Spelling

(For more information about spelling, see pp. 143-148.)

1. It's alright to be patient.
2. A golfer needs a bag, clubs, balls, ect.
3. It's none of your buisness.
4. Tommorow is Wendsday and the start of Febuary.
5. Hamlet lets his depth of greif be known in the first solioquay.
6. Alot of us aren't sure.
7. She see's the childern.
8. She was a mischievious girl.
9. I beleive their seperation was embarassing.
10. It is neccessary to go to the restraunt.
11. My dog frequently burys his toyes under the tree.
12. To practice that kind of deciet, you have to be a theif.
13. Thier going to an eatery for desert.
14. In the play, he was called a scoundrel and a nave.
15. It ocurred once, but it won't happen again.

(For answers, see p. 168.)

Punctuation

(For more information about punctuation, see pp. 149-153.)

1. I'm not sure if I want to, it's bound to be expensive.

2. May I leave.

3. I want two things for Christmas — a new train set and a Nintendo game.

4. My birthday is in June, his is in December.

5. There are two main characters in the story Paul and his father.

6. He said sure you can.

7. In fact it was summer.

8. At the end of the play the students applauded.

9. She brought to the party some cheese some crackers and some pickles.

10. Before we leave we should feed the dogs and water the plants.

11. Its bound to happen sooner or later Mollys car will win the race.

12. The coach screamed Do it now

13. The plane stops in Kelowna Kamloops and Prince George.

14. My uncle a famous writer recently won a prize for his work.

15. His reason for not coming a sore stomach.

(For answers, see p. 169.)

Capitalization and Titles

(For more information about capitalization and titles, see p. 154.)

1. in rome, early christians worshipped god in secret.

2. The story gives readers Faith and Hope.

3. the greeks worshipped zeus, their chief god.

4. The british have good soccer players in england.

5. We studied hamlet.

6. Check the icelandic poppies.

7. Read the tell-tale heart, a short story by edgar allan poe.

8. When the money is found, tony says its margot's.

9. We met prime minister chretien.

10. After visiting relatives on the east coast, we will drive south.

11. For whom the bell tolls by Ernest hemingway was first published in english.

12. Surprising as it may seem, french is not danielle's first language.

13. James joyce wrote araby, which is a very famous short story.

14. Citizen kane is thought by many critics to be one of the great films of the twentieth century.

15. The article, camp hernia, appeared in the national post.

(For answers, see p. 170.)

A Review of Common Errors

1. They drove over in there new car.

2. We tried to find a set of antique glasses for their wedding present however we could only find antique silver goblets.

3. There are three things I want for Christmas a new set of dishes, a set of dessert bowls, and a set of coffee mugs.

4. Do you want the snow cleared off your roof.

5. Hamlet fools his friends, deceives his girlfriend, and insulted his father-in-law.

6. Its not good to be to late.

7. On new year's eve, she proposed a toast for world piece.

8. She pretend that she was unhappy.

9. He pushed Alan to far.

10. Their are three things I need. Flour, sugar, and chocolate.

11. We wanted to holiday at Christmas however we couldn't afford to go anywhere.

12. He truely loves working for the goverment.

13. She is a women who knows alot about Love.

14. *Boys and Girls* is a good short story.

15. I am kinda sad.

16. He wrote the final exam at the end of June in July he went on a month-long holiday.

17. Know one she knew has been in the room all morning.

18. We snuck into the show.

19. Elmer was stubborn, ill-mannered rascal.

20. Darla's car failed the emissions inspection it had to be take to a garage for some expensive work.

21. In my opinion we must have more community facilities and more services for the elderly.

22. The Oilers could of won the fights if they weren't such wimps.

23. The mens' hats are on the table.

24. Listen to the fathers suggestion.

25. Fidos collar was rough and scratched its neck.

26. Dogs don't just here there names they know more then one word.

27. When she is in a hurry.

28. My Nintendo does not work good.

29. Your not making sense in you're situation.

30. She saved his butt.

31. If you do not hear from me by Friday.

32. She is a wonderful person, I know she will be a great asset to the organization.

33. Joseph Conrad is a fine writer, and anyone of their works will be an ideal topic for a term paper.

34. She travelled to Raymond's house by taking a westbound bus, would take a northernbound streetcar, and then could use light rapid transit.

35. No one cares if they miss the rap concert.

36. She is running for the chairman's position.

37. All together, the basketball team scored fifty points in the first half.

38. Can I have a second helping of mashed potatoes?

39. She stoped the neumatic drill to hear what the boss had to say.

40. Dans reading of shakespeares play as you like it is far fetched.

(For answers, see p. 171.)

ANSWERS TO EXERCISES

Answers may vary.

Answers to Sentence Errors

1. Doubling ensures your safety.

2. When my family has reunions, we have a good time.

3. When she felt lonely, she would write. In fact, writing was her salvation.
   or When she felt lonely, she would write; in fact, writing was her salvation.

4. They become more than roommates; they become brothers.

5. Paul breaks away from his father's technique, while Norman and the father keep casting the traditional way.

6. Conrad makes good progress, which is what makes it possible for him to survive his depression.

7. Swarn is friendly and kind; he has been very helpful to us.

8. Running down the road, the horse headed east.

9. He was friendly, kind, and decent, too.

10. There are other ways to solve problems, like discussing matters over tea.

11. The horse reared, whinnied, and bolted for the pasture.

12. The dog chased the possum along the fence until it caught the poor creature.

13. The shortstop fielded the baseball, bobbled it, and relayed the ball to first base.

14. I am the last person to ask for tax advice. I cannot even correctly add a column of numbers.

15. He is a competent painter, when he tries.

Answers to Agreement Problems

1. She is welcome to bring her own car.

2. Macbeth, not his wife, is plotting to kill King Duncan.

3. Anybody who wants to start is welcome to do so.

4. She is a powerful woman.

5. Maggie liked to swim, ride, and play tennis.

6. Dustin, together with Richard and Omar, was given a raise.

7. A pencil and a ruler are useful tools.

8. The team is up for the game; it might win.

9. One should remember to phone one's parents.

10. The whole family is upset.

11. When the average Canadian complains about taxes, he or she says that no one cares.

12. Although a pocket thesaurus is useful, it cannot replace a standard desk thesaurus.

13. The bug's antennae are severely bent.

14. A list of the required books, along with the timetable, is included.

15. The whole committee is infuriated.

Answers to Word Choice

1. I went to see the doctor because of my bad cold.

2. He was the man who lost his dog.

3. When one looks beneath the surface of the poem, one can see that the author or speaker is concerned with death.

4. She becomes insane. *or* She loses her sanity.

5. She changes her mind; she wants a career.

6. Maybe the boy isn't getting the attention he needs.

7. The poppies are new flowers. *or* The poppy is a new flower.

8. This movie is weak. *or* This movie isn't very good.

9. Hitler was an evil man.

10. The boy's comment could have revealed prejudice.

11. You can see the comedian's face in every newspaper across Canada.

12. The detergent is the best cleanser known to humans.

13. Victoria has less rain than Prince Rupert.

14. If you master all the components of the program, you will certainly be able to write well.

15. The pipes, which are in the garage, need to be organized according to size.

Answers to Homophones

1. There was no one there except the staff.

2. Are you already finished?

3. He was under the illusion that he was earning twenty-five dollars an hour.

4. They're coming inside with their umbrellas.

5. He couldn't bear to leave his family long.

6. Romar was on board the plane by one o'clock.

7. The old car was a sight for sore eyes.

8. Did you ever hear of anything so absurd?

9. You're certain?

10. Before you buy your new car, you should get some insurance.

11. Who is the principal of your school?

12. As a basketball guard, she has no peer.

13. In the provincial museum, one is not allowed to shout.

14. The Queen has witnessed many changes in Canada during her reign.

15. The lone robber made her getaway from the bank.

Answers to Spelling

1. It's all right to be patient.

2. A golfer needs a bag, clubs, balls, etc.

3. It's none of your business.

4. Tomorrow is Wednesday and the start of February.

5. Hamlet lets his depth of grief be known in the first soliloquy.

6. A lot of us aren't sure.

7. She sees the children.

8. She was a mischievous girl.

9. I believe their separation was embarrassing.

10. It is necessary to go to the restaurant.

11. My dog frequently buries his toys under the tree.

12. To practise that kind of deceit, you have to be a thief.

13. They're going to an eatery for dessert.

14. In the play, he was called a scoundrel and a knave.

15. It occurred once, but it won't happen again.

Answers to Punctuation

1. I'm not sure if I want to; it's bound to be expensive.

2. May I leave?

3. I want two things for Christmas: a new train set and a Nintendo game.

4. My birthday is in June; his is in December.

5. There are two main characters in the story: Paul and his father.

6. He said, "Sure, you can."

7. In fact, it was summer.

8. At the end of the play, the students applauded.

9. She brought to the party some cheese, some crackers, and some pickles.

10. Before we leave, we should feed the dogs and water the plants.

11. It's bound to happen sooner or later. Molly's car will win the race.

12. The coach screamed, "Do it now!"

13. The plane stops in Kelowna, Kamloops, and Prince George.

14. My uncle, a famous writer, recently won a prize for his work.

15. His reason for not coming: a sore stomach.

1. In Rome, early Christians worshipped God in secret.

2. The story gives readers faith and hope.

3. The Greeks worshipped Zeus, their chief god.

4. The British have good soccer players in England.

5. We studied *Hamlet*.

6. Check the Icelandic poppies.

7. Read "The Tell-Tale Heart," a story by Edgar Allan Poe.

8. When the money is found, Tony says it's Margot's.

9. We met Prime Minister Chrétien.

10. After visiting relatives on the East Coast, we will drive south.

11. *For Whom the Bell Tolls* by Ernest Hemingway was first published in English.

12. Surprising as it may seem, French is not Danielle's first language.

13. James Joyce wrote "Araby," which is a very famous short story.

14. *Citizen Kane* is thought by many critics to be one of the great films of the twentieth century.

15. The article, "Camp Hernia," appeared in the *National Post*.

1. They drove over in their new car.

2. We tried to find a set of antique glasses for their wedding present; however, we could only find antique silver goblets.

3. There are three things I want for Christmas: a new set of dishes, a set of dessert bowls, and a set of coffee mugs.

4. Do you want the snow cleared off your roof?

5. Hamlet fools his friends, deceives his girlfriend, and insults his father-in-law.

6. It's not good to be too late.

7. On New Year's Eve, she proposed a toast for world peace.

8. She pretended that she was unhappy.

9. He pushed Alan too far.

10. There are three things I need: flour, sugar, and chocolate.

11. We wanted to holiday at Christmas; however, we couldn't afford to go anywhere.

12. He truly loves working for the government.

13. She is a woman who knows a lot about love.

14. "Boys and Girls" is a good short story.

15. I am sad. *or* I am kind of sad.

16. He wrote the final exam at the end of June. In July, he went on a month-long holiday.

17. No one she knew has been in the room all morning.

18. We sneaked into the show.

19. Elmer was a stubborn, ill-mannered rascal.

20. Darla's car failed the emissions inspection; it had to be taken to a garage for some expensive work.

21. In my opinion, we must have more community facilities and more services for the elderly.

22. The Oilers could have won the fights if they weren't such cowards.

23. The men's hats are on the table.

24. Listen to the father's suggestion.

25. Fido's collar was rough and scratched its neck.

26. Dogs don't just hear their names; they know more than one word.

27. When she is in a hurry, she makes mistakes.

28. My Nintendo does not work well.

29. You're not making sense in your situation.

30. She saved his life.

31. If you do not hear from me by Friday, do not hesitate to call.

32. She is a wonderful person. I know she will be a great asset to the organization.

33. Joseph Conrad is a fine writer, and any one of his works will be an ideal topic for a term paper.

34. She travelled to Raymond's house by taking a westbound bus, a northbound streetcar, and the light rapid transit.

35. No one cares if he or she misses the rap concert.

36. She is running for the chairperson's position.

37. Altogether, the basketball team scored fifty points in the first half.

38. Can I have a second helping of mashed potatoes?

39. She stopped the pneumatic drill to hear what the boss had to say.

40. Dan's reading of Shakespeare's play *As You Like It* is far-fetched.

Glossary

Abbreviation

An abbreviation is a shortened form of a word or phrase. There is a trend away from using periods in many abbreviations, especially names of companies or organizations. While abbreviations are useful in lists, tables, footnotes, and technical documents, most are inappropriate in formal writing.

A few exceptions are:

- titles, such as Mrs., Mr., and Dr.
- St. for Saint in place names
- degrees and professional titles, such as Ph.D., B.A., C.A., when placed after a person's name
- indications of time, when used with figures, such as 7 p.m., A.D. 500

Acronym

An acronym is an artificial word formed from the first letter or first few letters of a group of words:

AIDS (*A*cquired *I*mmune *D*eficiency *S*yndrome)

sonar (*so*und *na*vigation and *r*anging)

Active and Passive Voice

A verb is in the active voice if its subject is the doer of the action. A verb is in the passive voice (*be* + past participle) when the subject of the verb receives the action:

Active: *The firefighters extinguished the fire.*

Passive: *The fire was extinguished.*

The passive voice allows the doer of the action to be omitted. Thus the doer may be unknown, unimportant, or obvious. Writers of scientific papers often prefer the passive voice: *the experiment was conducted.* Overuse of the passive voice, however, can weaken an argument; the active voice transmits a higher energy level and is usually clearer and more direct.

Adjective

An adjective (word, phrase, or clause) is used for the following:

- to modify a noun: *We heard a _loud_ noise. His _icy blue_ eyes stared at nothing.*
- to modify a pronoun: *_Poor_ me! She looked _pale_.*
- to answer the question what kind (*_sunny_ weather*),
  or how many (*_seven_ days*), or which one (*the _biggest_ book*)

Adverb

An adverb (word, phrase, or clause) is used for the following:

- to modify a verb: *He left the party _early_.*
- to modify an adjective: *Her face was _slightly_ pale.*
- to modify another adverb: *We left the party _very_ early.*
- to answer the question how (*I spoke _softly_*),
  or when (*I arrived _late_*), or where (*Move the chair _forward_*)

Agreement

SEE **Pronoun; Subject/Verb Agreement**

Antecedent

An antecedent is a noun or a noun phrase to which a pronoun refers:

Will the person who owns the red car please come to the office?

(*Person* is the antecedent of *who*.)

Owning a car has its drawbacks.

(*Owning a car* is the antecedent of *its*.)

Antonym

SEE **Synonym/Antonym**

Appositive

An appositive is a noun or a noun phrase that relates or explains a noun or pronoun that immediately precedes it. Appositives are set off with commas:

I am writing to Jane Saliani, <u>my best friend</u>.

Ms. Sharp, <u>the principal</u>, stood up.

Apostrophe [']

Use an apostrophe as follows:

- to show possession: *Jane's boat*
- to indicate a contraction: *don't, can't*
- to replace missing letters in speech: *"How 'bout you?"*
- to replace missing numbers in a date: class of '99
- to show the plural of letters or symbols: *There are three a's in Saskatchewan and two 9's in 1998.*

Article

The definite article, *the*, indicates that the following noun refers to something or someone in particular: *the book*. The indefinite article, *a* or *an*, indicates that the following noun is a member of a class: *a book of fiction*.

Auxiliary Verb

SEE **Verb**

Balance/Parallelism

Balance and parallelism are qualities of an essay in which like items are given similar treatment or weight. **Balance** generally refers to an aesthetic effect within the structure of an essay. Items that may be balanced include length of paragraphs or sections; weight given to particular ideas, arguments, or examples; and the treatments of these ideas, arguments, and examples in language. **Parallelism** is a more focussed term than balance, as it refers to the similar use of words, phrases, clauses, and sentences in like situations.

Bibliography/Works Cited

A bibliography is a list of all the works used in an essay, placed on a separate page at the end of the paper. Although there are variations in style, all bibliographies include the same basic information: the name of the author(s), the title of the work, and the name, date, and place of publication. Example: Smith, Allen Joseph. *Researching Your Family Tree.* Toronto: Gladhouse Press, 1998.

Capitalization

Capitalize the first letter, as follows:

- the first word in a sentence or a quotation:

  Here is one definition of a computer virus: "A dangerous program that can delete or scramble data or shut down your computer."

- the name of a particular person, place, or nation:

  My English penpal, Sterling Sawyer, will be visiting Canada this fall.

- the main words in a title:

  Roughing It in the Bush, Mathematics 201, Romeo and Juliet, O Canada

- titles and family relationships, when used as part of a person's name:

  I saw Dad go downstairs. (BUT _I saw my dad go downstairs._)

  Doctor Namis (BUT _the doctor_)

  Prime Minister Macdonald (BUT _the prime minister_)

- days of the week, months, and holidays:

  Tuesday; September; Ramadan

- organizations, political parties, religions:

  the United Nations; the Liberal Party; Judaism

- historical events, eras, and documents:

  the Seven Years War; the Great Depression; the BNA Act

Citation/Footnote

Citations or footnotes are used to acknowledge the sources of quotations, charts, tables, diagrams, and all ideas other than your own.

Clause

A clause is a group of related words that has a subject and a predicate.

- A **main** clause (also known as an **independent** clause or **principal** clause) expresses a complete thought and can stand alone as a sentence.

  A **subordinate** clause (also known as a **dependent** clause) does not express a complete thought and cannot stand alone as a sentence.

In the following examples, subordinate clauses are underlined.

- **adjective clause:**

  Marta, who sometimes looks after our dog, is going to veterinary college.

- **adverb clause:**

  When Riswan smiles, the whole room lights up.

- **co-ordinate clauses** (clauses of the same rank):

  You wash the dishes and I will dry them.

- **restrictive (essential) clauses** are not set off by commas:

  The book that I lent you belongs to my brother.

- **non-restrictive (non essential) clauses** are separated from the main clause by commas:

  The book, which doesn't belong to me, has to be returned today.

Cliché

Clichés are overworked expressions that no longer have much impact. They are best avoided. Examples: _free as a bird; sick as a dog; stay the course; between a rock and a hard place; last but not least; in the home stretch; under the weather._

Coherence

Coherence is a quality of writing in which the parts relate to each other clearly and logically. Coherence is related to unity, and is considered a principle of effective essay writing.

Colloquialism

A colloquialism is an expression that is used in informal conversation, but not in formal speech or writing.

Colon [:]

A colon warns you that something is to follow. Use colons in the following situations:

- to introduce a list:

    Colours have different meanings in western culture: red for danger, black for mourning, and white for purity.

- to introduce a quotation in formal writing:

    Kenneth Boulding described his vision of Canada in a memorable way: "Canada has no cultural unity, no linguistic unity, no religious unity, no economic unity, no geographic unity. All it has is unity."

- to express time: *8:45; 20:00*

- to separate the volume and page numbers of a magazine:

    Food Lovers Digest, 4:17-19

Comma [,]

A comma indicates a slight pause in a sentence. The common practice, especially in informal writing, to use as few commas as possible without obscuring the meaning. Use commas as follows:

- between clauses in compound sentences:

    Rula thought hard, but no solutions came to mind.

- with nouns of address:

    David, take the garbage out.

- with words, phrases, or clauses that interrupt a sentence:

    We will, nevertheless, do our best to win.

- with introductory words, phrases, or clauses:

    In the end, I stayed home and read.

- between items in a series:

    Jim, Walter, and Aviva work together at the factory.

    Note that some people omit the comma just before the *and* in a series. This is acceptable, as long as the use is consistent and it does not make the sentence unclear.

- in some forms of date: *January 14, 1997* (BUT *14 January 1997*)

- in addresses:

    Please send an information kit to
    Serge Laflamme, 334 Grosvenor Avenue, Montréal, Québec H3H 3C7
    Note that there is no comma before the postal code.

- between a city and a country: *Ottawa, Canada*

- in salutations of personal letters: *Dear Sam,*

- to set off degrees and titles:

    Peter Mishinski, Ph.D.; Lorraine Markotic, M.P.

Comma Splice

SEE **Run-on Sentence**

Comparative

SEE **Comparison**

Compare/Contrast

Comparing and contrasting are techniques to examine two or more subjects for their similarities and/or differences. Comparisons emphasize similarities; contrasts emphasize differences.

Comparison

The forms of an adjective or adverb that indicate degrees in quality, quantity, or manner. The degrees are:

- **positive:** *black, easy, dangerous, good; soon, slowly, badly*
- **comparative:** *blacker, easier, more dangerous, better; sooner, more slowly, worse*
- **superlative:** *blackest, easiest, most dangerous, best; soonest, most slowly, worst*

Compound Word

A compound word is a combination of two or more words. Some compound words are written as one word (*hotline*), some are hyphenated (*hang-gliding*), and some are written as separate words (*check mark*).

Conjunction

A conjunction is a word that connects words, phrases, or clauses, and indicates the relationship between them.

- A **co-ordinating** conjunction connects two words, phrases, or clauses of equal rank:

  I would like to go to the concert, <u>but</u> I have no money.

- A **subordinating** conjunction connects a subordinate clause to a main clause:

  I break out in hives <u>whenever</u> I eat pickles.

Connective

A connective is a word that joins words, phrases, or clauses. Connectives are usually conjunctions, prepositions, and relative pronouns.

Connotation/Denotation

Connotation and denotation are two categories or levels of meaning. The denotation of a word is its literal, basic, dictionary meaning. The connotation of a word refers to an additional or figurative meaning.

Context

Context is the personal, social, or historical circumstances or background that needs to be known if a reader is to appreciate fully the significance of a work. The context of World War II and the Holocaust may be necessary for a story set in the 1940s.

Contraction

A contraction is a shortened form of a word or words in which an apostrophe shows where letters have been omitted: *don't = do not; I've = I have; there's = there is.*

Critical Response

Critical response usually refers to a serious examination of a topic or literary work for its own sake, without reference to personal views, biasses, values, or beliefs. A critical reading does not use first person pronouns and aims to be objective and neutral in its presentation of ideas and supporting evidence.

SEE ALSO **Personal Response**

Dangling Modifier

SEE **Misplaced Modifier**

Dash (—)

A dash marks a strong break in a sentence:

It wasn't until Friday — or it may have been Saturday — that I discovered my wallet was missing.

Did you ever see the film — but no, it was made before you were born.

Three students — Ruby, Amina, and Michael — were named as finalists.
Jack works hard — when he has to.

Dashes are useful for emphasis. However, using many dashes can make your writing disjointed and difficult to read. Consider using other punctuation instead.

Diction

Diction refers to the manner of expressing ideas in words. Good diction includes grammatical correctness, a wide vocabulary, and skill in the choice of effective words.

Direct Speech

In direct speech (also called direct quotation), the words spoken are quoted directly, in quotation marks: *"Who's been using my computer?" asked the girl.*

In indirect speech (also called indirect quotation), no quotation marks are necessary. The words written are not exactly the same as the words spoken: *The girl asked who had been using her computer.*

Double Negative

Using two negative words (such as *not* and *never*) in the same sentence creates a double negative. Avoid confusion by removing or replacing one of the two words. Double negatives are often created in sentences where the word *not* is hidden in a contraction, such as *can't, won't,* or *don't.*

Confusing: *I can't barely see!*

Better: *I can barely see!* OR *I can't see!*

Emphasis

Emphasis is the stressing or calling attention to important ideas in a sentence, a paragraph, or an essay. Emphasis can be given through the placement of an idea, a repetition, an elaboration, and so on.

Euphemism

A euphemism is a word or expression that is meant to blunt the impact of harsh or unacceptable words or phrases. Some common euphemisms are: *pass away; senior citizen; rest room; special needs.* As the military use of terms like *collateral damage* instead of *deaths* shows, there can be a fine line between using a euphemism and obscuring the truth. As a general rule, the direct way to say something is usually best.

Exclamation Mark [!]

An exclamation mark gives emphasis, and expresses surprise, delight, or alarm: *Hey! How sweet! Watch out!* Most writers trust their words to express whatever mood or emotion they wish to convey. When used sparingly, exclamation marks can be helpful, but too many may weaken their effect.

Exposition

Exposition is a type of prose, or vehicle, in which the author's purpose is to explain through a presentation of ideas focussing on a particular topic.

Footnote

SEE **Citation/Footnote**

Formal/Informal Language
- **Formal** language is a more serious style used in situations such as essays and prepared speeches, in which ideas are presented to an audience. It uses a tone more elevated and careful than conversation. It follows rules of grammar closely and uses crafted diction and sentences. Although it is mature and dignified, there is no need for formal English to be stiff, pompous, or artificial. Formal English is employed in business and technical writing, public speeches, editorials, sermons, textbooks, and literary criticism written by students. It generally avoids first person pronouns (*I-me-mine-my*), and contractions.
- **Informal** language is a more relaxed, casual style such as the way in which people commonly speak. It is used in informal communications such as e-mail, friendly letters, advertising, magazines of general interest, and much of literature, especially personal narratives and personal essays. Vocabulary, word choice, and sentences tend to be less structured for purposeful effect. Tone is often light and may be humorous in contrast to more serious formal language. Informal style allows the use of everyday phrases, idioms, contractions, and first person pronouns.

Gerund
A gerund is the form of a verb that ends in *ing*, used as a noun:

Dancing is my favourite exercise.

Helping Verb
SEE **Verb**

Homophone
Homophones are words that are pronounced the same but have different meanings, such as *see* and *sea*. The following homophones are often confused: *complement/compliment; hear/here; its/it's; passed/past; piece/peace; principal/principle; their/they're/there; to/too/two; through/threw; who's/whose; your/you're*. If you are unsure of the correct spelling, check your dictionary. SEE ALSO pages 126-141, **Commonly Confused Words**

Hyphen [-]
Use hyphens in the following way:
- in compound numbers between 21 and 99: *twenty-one*
- in time: *the five-fifteen bus*
- in fractions: *one-half of a pie*
- in some numerical expressions: *a ten-year-old boy; a twenty-dollar bill*
- to divide a word between syllables at the end of a line:
  dis-satisfied; dissat-isfied; dissatis-fied

Note that as there are many exceptions to these rules, it is safest to check your dictionary for guidance.

Idiom
An idiom is a colourful word, phrase, or expression which is used and easily understood by people speaking the same language. Some examples in English are *catch a cold, he's a pain in the neck, how do you do, to take after one's mother*. These combinations often seem odd or puzzling to people from cultures not speaking the same language, because the meaning of the idiom is different from the literal meaning of the words.

Imperative
SEE **Mood**

Indefinite Adjective

An indefinite adjective indicates an unspecified person or thing: *another, each, much, any, some, such.* Note that these words also act as pronouns.

Indefinite Pronoun

An indefinite pronoun refers to an unspecified person or thing: *anything, nobody, someone.*

Indicative

SEE **Mood**

Infinitive

The infinitive is the form of a verb usually introduced by *to*. It is often used as a noun: *To exercise makes good sense.*

SEE ALSO **Split Infinitive**

Informal Language

SEE **Formal/Informal Language**

Interjection

An interjection is a word that shows emotion, and often involves an exclamation mark: *Oh, you scared me!* Some other interjections are: *ah, hello, hey, oops, ouch, no, yes.*

Interrogatives

Interrogatives are the words used in asking questions.

- Interrogative adverbs are *where, when, why, how,* and their compounds *wherever,* etc.
- Interrogative pronouns are *who, which, what,* and their compounds *whoever,* etc.

Intransitive Verb

SEE **Verb**

Irregular Verb

SEE **Verb**

Jargon

Jargon is the specialized language of a particular group, or occupation. Authors strive for clarity and precision in their diction by considering the appropriateness of any specialized language (e.g., medical jargon) to their audience, and by questioning the clarity and legitimacy of their word choices.

Linking verb

SEE **Verb**

Metaphor and Simile

Metaphors and similes are both forms of comparison.

- A simile compares two things or ideas using *like* or *as: The icicles looked like bony fingers, pointing down at him accusingly.*
- A metaphor makes the comparison implicitly, without using *like* or *as: Bony fingers of ice pointed down at him accusingly.*

SEE ALSO **Cliché**

Modifier

A modifier is a word, phrase, or clause that qualifies the meaning of a word.

- A **misplaced** modifier appears to modify the wrong word or words because it is too far from what it modifies. For example, _She watched the sun rise from her balcony_ has a misplaced modifier. It seems to say that the sun was rising from the balcony. A better sentence would be: _From her balcony, she watched the sun rise._

- A **dangling** modifier occurs when the word being modified does not appear in the sentence: _While on holiday, a thief broke into our house_ seems to say the thief was on holiday. A better sentence would be: _While we were on holiday, a thief broke into our house._

Mood

Mood is the feeling that is created in the reader, listener, or viewer of a literary work, performance, or movie. In most language situations such as a short story or a poem, the mood is created by words, images, dialogue, description, narration, and local colour.

SEE ALSO **Tone**

Mood (of a verb)

The mood of a verb shows the manner of the action. There are three moods.

- The **indicative** mood states a fact or asks a question: _She wrote an essay. Did she write an essay?_

- The **imperative** mood gives a command or makes a request: _Write an essay. Please write an essay._

- The **subjunctive** mood is used in subordinate clauses, to express doubt or possibility: _If she were to write an essay, ..._

Noun

A noun is a word that refers to people, places, qualities, things, actions, or ideas: _When Joe was at the library in St. John's, curiosity enticed him to read an article that claimed fear could be cured by meditation._ There are four main types of noun:

- **abstract noun:** _happiness, beauty._
- **collective noun:** _class, herd, bunch_
- **concrete noun:** _hand, butterfly, birthday party, examination_
- **proper noun:** _Janice, Edmonton, December._ Proper nouns begin with a capital letter.

Number

The number of a noun, pronoun, or verb shows whether it is singular (one thing) or plural (more than one):

- singular: _She is a happy child._
- plural: _They are happy children._

Object

English has three types of objects. In the following examples, the direct object is in bold type, and the indirect object is underlined.

- A **direct object** is a noun or pronoun that answers the question what? or who? about the verb: _He bought a **kite**._

- An **indirect object** answers the question to what?, to whom?, for what?, or for whom? about the verb: _He bought me a **kite**._

- The **object of a preposition** is a noun or pronoun that comes at the end of a phrase that begins with a preposition: _He bought a **kite** for me._

Objective/Subjective

Objective and subjective are possible approaches of a writer. A writer who approaches a topic objectively will present facts and deal in the observable world. However, the writer might approach the same topic subjectively by presenting only her or his own thoughts and feelings. Much writing falls between the two extremes of personal opinion and support from scientific studies. Some topics cannot be addressed solely through observable facts; when this is the case, the writer often attempts to be as objective as possible by, for example, presenting opposing opinions, stating assumptions and personal biasses, and so on. Reportage tends to be objective in comparison with intentionally subjective news articles, or personal essays.

Paragraph

A paragraph is a group of sentences that develop one aspect of a topic, or one phase of a narrative. The sentences in a paragraph should be clearly related to each other. Sometimes, especially in essays, the aspect or point being developed is expressed in a **topic sentence**, and the other sentences in the paragraph expand on this statement.

Parallel Structure

In a sentence, two or more elements that are of equal importance, expressed in similar grammatical terms to emphasize their relationship, are called parallel. Sentences without parallel structure can sound both confusing and awkward. Parallel structure is especially important in lists; with expressions like *both...and, not only...but also, whether...or, either...or;* and in words, phrases, or clauses joined by *and*.

Not Parallel: *Campers are taught hiking, swimming, and how to canoe.*

Parallel: *Campers are taught to hike, swim, and canoe.* OR

Campers are taught hiking, swimming, and canoeing.

Parallelism

SEE **Balance/Parallelism**

Parentheses [( )]

- Use parentheses to set off comments or asides in a sentence: *They lived happily ever after (and so did the dog).*
- When necessary, you can use punctuation marks within the parentheses, even if the parenthetical comment is in the middle of a sentence: *All of us except Peter (Peter is always optimistic!) were sure it was going to rain on our picnic.*
- You can place whole sentences in parentheses. If the sentence stands alone and is not grammatically related to the ones before and after it, punctuate the sentence within the parentheses as you would a regular sentence: *The French colony of Upper Volta, now called Burkina Faso, gained its independence in 1960. (Burkina Faso means "land of honest men.")*

Participle

A participle is a verb form that may be combined with auxiliary (helping) verbs to form different tenses, or can act alone as an adjective.

- The regular **present participle** ends in *ing*:
  We <u>are moving</u> to Calgary; a <u>moving</u> target
- The regular **past participle** ends in *ed*:
  You <u>have spoiled</u> my day; a <u>spoiled</u> child

Part of Speech

A part of speech is one of the eight classes into which words are grouped according to their uses in a sentence: adjective, adverb, conjunction, interjection, noun, preposition, pronoun, and verb.

Period [.]

Use a period:

- to mark the end of a sentence: *The sky is blue.*
- after abbreviations and initials: *J.J. Cale; Mr.; St.*

Person

The person of a word indicates whether a someone is speaking (first person), is being spoken to (second person), or is being spoken about (third person).

Personal pronouns and verbs change their forms to show person.

- first person: *I listen to music. We listen to music.*
- second person: *You listen to music.*
- third person: *He/she listens to music. They listen to music.*

Personal Response

In a personal response, the reader/listener/viewer responds to a topic or literary selection as an individual presenting personal views, opinions, beliefs, and values. The respondent mentions past experiences (of his/her own, or of others personally or not personally known), prior knowledge, memories and associations, and makes observations based on what is personally known about a subject. Personal response, then, is concerned with establishing relevance between the work or topic and the respondent. Literary and critical views are not the main focus, therefore, in a personal response.

SEE ALSO **Critical Response**

Phrase

A phrase is a group of words that does not contain a subject and a verb. Note that categories of phrases overlap — a prepositional phrase can also be an adjective phrase, etc.

- A **noun phrase** acts as a noun:
  She wants to go swimming.
- An **adjective phrase** acts as an adjective:
  Moving fast, I shut the door.
- An **adverb phrase** acts as an adverb:
  Marcel spoke for the first time.
- A **prepositional phrase** contains a preposition, and acts as a noun, an adjective, or an adverb:
  From my house to yours is only three blocks. (noun)
  The books in the library are for everyone to use. (adjectives)
  I accept your invitation with great pleasure. (adverb)

Plagiarism

Plagiarism is the process of borrowing the exact words, ideas, or writing of someone else and passing them off as one's own. Considered theft because a writer's property has been used without permission, plagiarism is a serious academic offence in schools, universities, and colleges.

Prefix

A prefix is a word or syllable added on to the beginning of a word to make a new word. For example, *dis-* added to *appear* makes *disappear*. Often, knowing what a prefix means can help you to figure out the meaning of a new word. Here is a list of some common prefixes and their meanings:

a- (not)	*mal-* (bad)
ante- (before)	*mis-* (wrong)
anti- (against)	*mono-* (one)
multi- (many)	*non-* (not)
bi- (two)	*post-* (after)
circum- (around)	*pseudo-* (false)
co- (together)	*re-* (again)
dis- (not)	*retro-* (back)
extra- (beyond)	*semi-* (half)
fore- (before)	*super-* (over)
hyper- (excessively)	*trans-* (across)
in- (not)	*tri-* (three)
inter- (between; among)	*un-* (not)
	uni- (one)

Preposition

A preposition is a word that shows the relationship between a noun or pronoun (called the object of the preposition) and some other word in the sentence. A preposition and its object make up a prepositional phrase: *The house in the valley was swept away by the flood.* Some words that can act as prepositions are: *at, by, from, for, in, on, to, with.*

Pronoun Usage

A pronoun is a word that replaces a noun or another pronoun. There are many different types of pronouns, and most of them cause no problems. However, there are a few pitfalls.

- It should be clear what word the pronoun replaces (its antecedent). Here are some examples of sentences with unclear antecedents.

  Unclear: *Linda loves looking after Sandra, because she is so good.*

  Clear: *Linda loves looking after Sandra, because Sandra is so good.*

- Usually you will have no trouble choosing the right form of a personal pronoun. However, pay attention when the pronoun is joined to another noun or pronoun by *and, or,* or *nor.* Use the form of the pronoun that you would use if the other noun or pronoun were not there:

  Incorrect: *Neither John nor me had done the work.*

  (*me had done* is wrong)

  Correct: *Neither John nor I had done the work.*

  (*I had done* is correct)

  Incorrect: *Ms. Singh read the book to Saritsa and I.*

  (*read the book to I* is wrong)

  Correct: *Ms. Singh read the book to Saritsa and me.*

  (*read the book to me* is correct)

- When you use a personal pronoun immediately after a form of the verb *be* (*am, is, are, was, were, had been, will be,* etc.), you use the object form when you are talking: *It is me.*

  However, in formal language, it is more correct to use the subject case: *It is I who did all the work.*

- Personal pronouns (*I, me, you, they, us,* etc.) should agree in number and gender with the noun or pronoun they replace:

  Incorrect: *A <u>clown</u> always looks happy, even if <u>they</u> are crying inside.*

  Better: *<u>Clowns</u> always look happy, even if <u>they</u> are crying inside.*
- When an indefinite pronoun (*any, every, some, each, all,* etc.) is the subject of a verb, the verb should agree in number with the pronoun. Some pronouns are singular (*each, either,* etc.), some are plural (*few, many,* etc.), and some can be singular or plural (*most, some,* etc.): *Most of the pie is gone. Most of the people are gone.*
- A pronoun that refers to an indefinite pronoun should also agree with the indefinite pronoun in number and gender:

  Everyone who is going on the trip should bring his or her own lunch. (*everyone* is singular, so the pronouns *his* or *her* must be singular)
- Sometimes the pronouns *we* and *us* are used just before a noun. In sentences like the following examples, check that you are using the right form of the pronoun by reading the sentence without the following noun, to see if it is correct:

  Incorrect: *Us dog lovers love to talk about our pets.*

             (*Us love* is wrong)

  Correct: *We dog lovers love to talk about our pets.*

             (*We love* is correct)

Punctuation

Punctuation marks are used to indicate relationships between words, phrases, and clauses. See individual entries for punctuation marks in this glossary.

Question Mark [?]

A question mark indicates a direct question: *Where is the remote?* (BUT *Sasha asked where the remote was.*)

Redundancy

Redundancy is the use of unnecessary words in a sentence:

Redundant: *I woke up at 7:30 a.m. in the morning.*

Better: *I woke up at 7:30 a.m.*

Redundant: *The reason I stayed home is because I was sick.*

Better: *I stayed home because I was sick.*

Run-on Sentence

- A run-on sentence is formed when two sentences are run into one. To fix a run-on sentence, add the proper punctuation, or change the wording to make it a single sentence:

  Run-on: *The sky is clear it is spring at last.*

  Better: *The sky is clear; it is spring at last.* OR *The sky is clear, and it is spring at last.* OR *The sky is clear because it is spring at last.*
- Two sentences separated only by a comma is called a comma splice. Fix a comma splice the same way you would fix a run-on sentence.

Semicolon [;]

- Use a semicolon to separate two related independent clauses: *I love watching television after school; it relaxes me.*
- Semicolons are used to separate items in a list, when one or more of the items contains a comma: *Walter has lived in Tokyo, Japan; London, England; and Estevan, Saskatchewan.*

Sentence

A sentence is a group of words representing a complete thought. It contains a subject and a predicate.

- A **simple sentence** consists of one main clause: *He entered the room.*
- A **compound sentence** consists of two or more main clauses: *He entered the room and then he sat down.*
- A **complex sentence** consists of one main clause and one or more subordinate clauses: *While I watched, he entered the room.*
- A **compound-complex sentence** consists of two main clauses and one or more subordinate clauses: *While I watched, he entered the room and sat down.*

Sentence Fragment

A sentence fragment is a group of words that is set off like a sentence, but that lacks either a verb or a subject. Sentence fragments are acceptable in dialogue, spoken English, and sometimes in informal writing, but are not appropriate in formal writing.

Fragment: *We went to the game on Saturday. Just Josh and I.*
                    (lacks a verb)
Revised: *Just Josh and I went to the game on Saturday.*
Fragment: *Never did understand those engines.*
                    (lacks a subject)
Revised: *I never did understand those engines.*

Slang

Slang is colourful informal language appropriate in current conversation especially with friends, but avoided altogether in formal language situations. Slang is coined because of people's search for novelty and originality and is used by people to show how up-to-date they are. Ironically, slang ends up getting overused, quickly becomes stale or passé, and dies out. Examples of dead slang words from the past forty years include: *groovy, rad, dude, rip-off, bad scene.*

Split Infinitive

Split infinitives occur when an adverb is put between *to* and the verb: *to boldly go where no one has gone before.* Although split infinitives are not necessarily wrong, awkward ones should be avoided: *After a while I was able to, although not very accurately, distinguish the good customers from the bad* would be better as *After a while I was able to distinguish, although not very accurately, the good customers from the bad.*

Subject

The subject of a sentence is the word, phrase, or clause that names the person, place, or thing about which something is said: *The doctor said that I need rest. Whoever holds the winning ticket has not claimed the prize. When will the concert start?*

Subject/Verb Agreement

A verb should always agree in number with its subject. Singular subjects take singular verbs, and a plural subject takes a plural verb. Here are some tips:

- Prepositional phrases like *at school, under my desk, through the woods, with great sadness, of the cars* never contain the subject of a sentence:

  Wrong: *One of the cars were stolen.*

               (*cars* is not the subject)

  Corrected: *One of the cars was stolen.*

               (the subject *one* needs a singular verb)

- *There* is not usually the subject of the verb:

  There are many reasons why I like you.

  (subject is *reasons*)

  There is my workbook.

  (subject is *workbook*)

- If the subject has two parts, joined by *or, not either...or, or neither...nor,* make the verb agree with the part of the subject nearest to it:

  Neither my brother nor <u>my parents were</u> at my recital.

  Neither my brother nor <u>my sister was</u> at my recital.

- Some subjects look like they are plural, but they are really singular: <u>The Diviners</u> *is a remarkable book. <u>The news is</u> about to come on. <u>Five dollars is</u> not enough to go to a movie.*

Subjective

SEE **Objective/Subjective**

Suffix

A suffix is a syllable or letters added to the end of a word to make a new word. Knowing the meaning of some common suffixes can help you to figure out the meaning of new words.

-able (able to/inclined to/causing): *agreeable; capable; comfortable*

-er (more/one who does): *delightful*

-ish (belonging to/having the qualities of/somewhat): *English; boyish; blueish*

-ize (cause to become/become/affect): *caramelize; crystallize*

-less (without/not able to): *loveless; countless*

-ly (in a certain manner): *kindly*

-ment (state, condition, or result of): *abandonment*

-ness (state, condition, or result of): *awareness*

Superlative

SEE **Comparison**

Syllable

One or more letters that represent one sound. There are four syllables in *differently: dif-fer-ent-ly.*

Synonym

Synonyms are words that mean the same thing, although they differ in the shade of meaning they imply. For example, *discuss, talk,* and *chat* can all be said to mean more or less the same thing, but each has a different connotation: *The council discussed the proposal at length. The speaker talked for twenty minutes. Eli chatted to me on the phone.* Antonyms are words that mean the opposite. For example, antonyms for *hate* could be *love, enjoy, like,* etc. When choosing the right word for a particular context, check in your dictionary or thesaurus.

Syntax

Syntax is the arrangement of words to form sentences, clauses, or phrases; It is also called sentence structure.

Tense

The tense of a verb is the property that expresses time. English has five categories of tense: **present, past, future, perfect,** and **progressive.** The progressive and perfect tenses may combine with each other and with the present, past, or future tense to form compound tenses.

present:	*they try*
past:	*they tried*
future:	*they will try*
present perfect:	*they have tried*
past perfect:	*they had tried*
future perfect:	*they will have tried*
present progressive:	*they are trying*
past progressive:	*they were trying*
future progressive:	*they will be trying*
etc.	

Thesis/Thesis Statement

The thesis is the main idea, position, or view of the essay writer, and the thesis statement is its expression in a statement. In an essay, the thesis is stated directly, usually in the opening paragraph. Often, though, in fiction, drama, or poetry, the thesis is implicit.

Tone

Tone is the attitude of a writer or presenter toward his or her own work or topic. Tone reveals how the author feels about the subject and may also reveal his or her underlying values and beliefs.

SEE ALSO **Mood**

Topic/Topic Sentence

The topic is the subject of the writing, and the topic sentence is its expression in a statement. The topic may be expressed both directly and indirectly, and it relates to the thesis of the writing. The topic of a portion of the writing may be called a subtopic.

Transitions

Transitions are words or phrases that link ideas, sentences, or paragraphs, making it easier for the reader to understand how parts of the essay relate. Transitions might emphasize structure, indicate time or location, highlight comparison or contrast, and so on.

Triteness

Triteness is the amateurish quality created by overuse of clichés or worn-out expressions such as *light of day, her better half,* and *raining cats and dogs.* Usually the trite expression has long lost its freshness and power because of over-repetition in everyday speech.

Unity

Unity is a quality of writing in which each part relates to a single purpose. Unity is related to coherence and is considered a principle of effective essay writing.

Verb

A verb is a word or phrase that expresses action or state of being: *I will write my essay this week. The weather was fine all day.* Choose colourful, exact verbs for high energy in your creative writing: *I burst into the room* has much more impact than *I walked into the room.*

- An **auxiliary** (helping) verb precedes its main verb and shows its tense, mood, and voice. Auxiliary verbs are: *be, do, have, can/could, may/might,* etc.

- A **transitive** verb requires an object to complete its meaning: *We value your opinion.*

- An **intransitive** verb does not require an object to complete its meaning: *The sun rises.*

- A **linking** verb connects a subject with a complement: *The shirt is red.* The most common linking verb is *be.* Good writers use the verb *to be* as little as possible, since it has a very low energy level. Instead of *The shirt is red*, say *The red shirt.*

- An **irregular** verb does not form its past tense or its past participle by adding *d* or *ed* to the infinitive form of the verb: *to sing*, past tense *sang*, past participle *sung*.

SEE ALSO **Mood (of a verb)**

Voice

SEE **Active and Passive Voice**

Works Cited

SEE **Bibliography/Works Cited**

Index